International conflicts of labour law

International conflicts of labour law

A survey of the law applicable to the international employment relation

Felice Morgenstern

International Labour Office   Geneva

ISBN 92-2-103593-X

First published 1984

LIPPINCOTT

K
7590
M67
1984

Printed in Switzerland

CONTENTS

Contents

LIST OF PERIODICAL PUBLICATIONS CITED
(Other than official gazettes and standard national law reports)

How cited:

Full title and place of publication:

Amer. J. Compar. Law	*The American Journal of Comparative Law* (Berkeley, California)
Amer. J. Int. Law	*The American Journal of International Law* (Washington, DC)
Ann. Inst. droit int.	*Annuaire de l'Institut de droit international* (Basle)
A.P.	Hueck-Nipperdey-Dietz, *Arbeitsrechtliche Praxis* (Munich)
Arbeit u. Recht	*Arbeit und Recht* (Cologne)
Arbeitsrecht in Stichworten	*Arbeitsrecht in Stichworten* (Bad Homburg)
A.W.D.	see under *R.I.W./A.W.D.*
Betr. Berat.	*Betriebs-Berater* (Heidelberg)
Br. Yearb. Int. Law	*British Yearbook of International Law* (London)
Bul. Czechoslovak Law	*Bulletin of Czechoslovak Law* (Prague)
Can. Yearb. Int. Law	*Canadian Yearbook of International Law* (Vancouver)
Clunet	*Journal du droit international* (Paris)
Cornell Int. Law J.	*Cornell International Law Journal* (Ithaca, New York)
Cours Acad. droit int.	*Recueil des cours de l'Académie de droit international de La Haye* (The Hague)
Dalloz-Sirey	*Recueil Dalloz-Sirey* (Paris)
Das Recht der Arbeit (Vienna)	*Das Recht der Arbeit* (Vienna)

Der Betrieb	*Der Betrieb* (Düsseldorf)
D° del trabajo	*Derecho del trabajo* (Buenos Aires)
Droit social	*Droit social* (Paris)
Droit travail et assur. chômage	*Droit du travail et assurance-chômage* (Berne)
F.E.P. Cases	*Fair Employment Practice Cases* (Washington, DC)
Industr. Law J.	*The Industrial Law Journal* (London)
Industr. Rel. Law Rep.	*Industrial Relations Law Reports* (London)
Int. Compar. Law Q.	*The International and Comparative Law Quarterly* (London)
Int. Labour Law Rep.	*International Labour Law Reports* (Alphen aan den Rijn, South Holland)
Int. Labour Rev.	*International Labour Review* (Geneva)
Int. Law Rep.	*International Law Reports* (London)
Int. Legal Materials	*International Legal Materials* (Washington, DC)
IPRspr.	*Die deutsche Rechtsprechung auf dem Gebiete des internationalen Privatrechts* (Tübingen)
J.C.P.	*La semaine juridique*, Juris-classeur Périodique (Paris)
J. Trib. Travail	*Journal des tribunaux du travail* (Brussels)
L.S.	*Legislative Series* of the International Labour Office (Geneva)
Neth. Yearb. Int. Law	*Netherlands Yearbook of International Law* (Alphen aan den Rijn, South Holland)
Neth. Int. Law Rev.	*Netherlands International Law Review* (Leyden)
N.J.W.	*Neue Juristische Wochenschrift* (Munich)
RabelsZ.	(Rabels) *Zeitschrift für ausländisches und internationales Privatrecht* (Tübingen)
Recht der Arbeit (Munich)	*Recht der Arbeit* (Munich)
Rev. crit.	*Revue critique de droit international privé* (Paris)
Rev. des sociétés	*Revue des sociétés* (Paris)
Rev. hell. droit int.	*Revue hellénique de droit international* (Athens)

Rev. trim. droit commercial	*Revue trimestrielle de droit commercial* (Paris)
Rev. trim. droit eur.	*Revue trimestrielle de droit européen* (Paris)
Riv. dir. int.	*Rivista di diritto internazionale* (Milan)
Riv. dir. int. priv. proc.	*Rivista di diritto internazionale privato e processuale* (Padua)
R.I.W./A.W.D. or, earlier, *A.W.D.*	*Recht der internationalen Wirtschaft (Aussenwirtschaftsdienst des Betriebs-Beraters)* (Heidelberg)
Scand. Studies in Law	*Scandinavian Studies in Law* (Stockholm)
Social and Labour Bul.	*Social and Labour Bulletin* of the International Labour Office (Geneva)
Travail et prof. d'outre-mer	*Travail et profession d'outre-mer* (Paris)
Yugoslav Law	*Yugoslav Law* (Belgrade)
Z. f. Arbeitsrecht	*Zeitschrift für Arbeitsrecht* (Cologne)
Z. f. ges. Handelsrecht	*Zeitschrift für das gesamte Handelsrecht* (Heidelberg)

INTRODUCTION

When a national of a particular country resides and works there in an employment relation entered into in that country with an employer who is a national of the same country, there is no doubt that the law of the country applies to every aspect of that relation. However, as soon as there is a foreign element (for example if the worker is a migrant, is under contract for work abroad or otherwise works outside the country of his nationality or normal residence, or if the employer is a foreign undertaking or a subsidiary of one) a question arises, namely which country's law should be applied to that employment or to particular aspects thereof. That question is not of interest only in the relatively rare cases in which disputes on the subject have to be dealt with by lawyers and courts. It is of daily relevance to undertakings that send workers abroad, have foreign subsidiaries or engage foreign labour; to workers' representatives in such undertakings and to unions bargaining with their management; to labour inspection services and other bodies concerned with the enforcement of labour law; and, of course, to the workers concerned.

The rules which determine the answers to the question are a part of what is a standard subject of study as private international law, or conflict of laws (i.e. conflicts between the laws of different "nations" or States, on the same subject).[1] Despite its name, private international law is a branch of national law. As will be seen, approaches to private international law vary greatly from country to country; so does labour law: the range of legal systems that may be affected by international employment relations is considerable. For reasons which should become apparent in Chapter I, it is not easy, even as regards the law of any single country, to be certain of the answers to all the issues which may be raised by employment relations with an international element; in a comparative study, all that can usefully be done is to indicate key problems and trends in their solution, and to seek to provide some guidance on the possible practical implications of those trends.

It has been suggested that differing approaches to the identification of the law applicable in labour matters are partly due to the fact that different types of employment abroad need to be treated differently. In particular, the movement of migrants from less developed to highly industrialised countries is seen as requiring solutions that are different from those called for by the assignment of workers away from the highly industrialised countries, often to the less developed. There are various sides to this question. In so far as the movements differ in such respects as duration and type of employment relation, there may be objective reasons for them to be governed by different rules. There may also be objective differences in bargaining power between different groups of workers. On the other hand, the superiority or otherwise of the labour law of one country to that of another may be a matter of purely subjective appreciation. No country has a monopoly of excellence in labour law; all that can be said is that in some countries certain aspects of such law are more favourable to the worker than they are in others: for example, the case law of European countries on the subject under consideration here shows that people happy to enjoy during service the terms of employment of a contract governed by United States law seek the protection of a European system of law when it comes to a problem of dismissal. A recent study [2] of the actual practice of a number of companies incorporated in the Federal Republic of Germany in sending workers abroad showed that those firms were anxious to exclude the applicability of certain aspects of the local law in the Middle East or North Africa (such as the payment of a thirteenth month of salary, or particularly generous leave provisions). Enforcement of whatever law is applicable is a different matter and has been a major concern to trade unions; [3] in so far as enforcement requires public supervision at the worksite, the mere existence of an international element does not in itself detract from the sole authority of the local authorities in that respect.

Not only do approaches differ from country to country, and reflect different types of foreign connections in labour matters. In many countries private international law is undergoing a wider process of evolution and reconsideration. There are two main reasons for this. On the one hand, on the national plane the law has to take account of growing state intervention in economic and social affairs; labour relations are one of the fields in which this factor is of considerable relevance. [4] On the other hand, internationally there has been a development of practices and institutions, including the growth of multinational groups of companies, which did not fit in with traditional concepts. [5] As a reflection of these developments, though not as a necessary result, the question is now also being asked in some countries whether private international law, which had traditionally been seen as providing a neutral method of choosing the system of law to govern a particular relation (i.e. a method treating all systems of law as equivalent), should not be so applied as to further social concepts, [6] in particular, by taking account in each case of the results of a choice of law.

The complexity of the subject makes it necessary to narrow it in two respects. First, the issues raised in private international law by individual and collective labour relations are not the same as those raised by social security, at any rate as regards national schemes; [7] therefore, while reference will be made in this study to some sources regarding the choice of law in social security, and to the criteria applied in that field, the subject will not be dealt with in any detail. Secondly, what is known as "international procedural law" (i.e. such matters as access to courts of one country or another and the manner of arranging for foreign law to be applied) will be touched upon only briefly.

Finally, a distinction should be made from the outset between the subject of this study, namely the determination of the law governing employment relations with an international aspect, and the treatment, in substantive law, of foreign workers. It may be that, in application of the principles to be considered below, a foreign worker hired for work in a country is subject to its law, but that rule does not prejudge whether the law in question may contain provisions regarding foreign workers which are different from those applicable to nationals. Conversely, the fact that countries of emigration seek, through model contracts or otherwise, to ensure minimum conditions for the employment of their nationals abroad in no way determines which law will govern all the aspects of employment that are not expressly agreed; the law in question may indeed decide the validity of the agreed terms themselves. It is therefore not proposed to duplicate here the considerable amount of material that has been published on the living and working conditions of migrants.

Notes

[1] There has been some academic controversy on whether the concept of "private" international law can embrace questions of choice of law in labour matters because many aspects of labour law are, in countries which make a distinction, considered to be "public" law. In 1971, members of the Institute of International Law considered that the concept of private international law could indeed embrace such questions (*Ann. Inst. droit int.*, 1971).

[2] H. Kronke: *Rechtstatsachen, kollisionsrechtliche Methodenentfaltung und Arbeitnehmerschutz im internationalen Arbeitsrecht* (Tübingen, 1980).

[3] For instance, at an ILO meeting of experts on the problems of foreign workers in the construction industry, held in October 1979, the Worker members proposed that there should be special agreements between home and host countries on inspection. A trade union seminar on an analogous subject held in Florence in September 1980 sought to make embassies and consular offices responsible for the protection of their nationals in employment abroad.

[4] See in particular S. Simitis: "Internationales Arbeitsrecht – Standort und Perspektiven", in *Festschrift für Gerhard Kegel* (Frankfurt am Main, 1977); and see the preamble to the resolution adopted by the Institute of International Law in 1975 on the application of foreign public law (*Ann. Inst. droit int.*, 1975).

[5] See the comments by R. H. Graveson, ibid., at p. 202.

[6] This development has been most marked in the United States, perhaps because most of the problems arise between the different states of a federation (see, on this, O. Kahn-Freund: "General problems of private international law", in *Cours Acad. droit int.*, 1974, III, pp. 139-474). However, in some Western European countries similar questions are being raised (for

instance, in the Federal Republic of Germany following Prof. K. Zweigert's article "Zur Armut des internationalen Privatrechts an sozialen Werten", in *RabelsZ.*, 1973, p. 435), and would appear to have influenced the drafters of the European Convention on the Law Applicable to Contractual Obligations (for an analysis of the Convention in this light, see H. Kronke: "Europäische Vereinheitlichung des Arbeitskollisionsrechts als Wirtschafts- und Sozialpolitik", in *RabelsZ.*, 1981, pp. 301-319).

[7] The problem posed by social security is essentially the delimitation and interplay of relevant legislation with a view to avoiding absence and duplication of coverage, and ensuring maintenance of rights; this is increasingly being achieved by international agreements.

SOURCES OF THE RELEVANT LAW

I

As already stated, private international law is a branch of national law. In principle its sources, particularly legislation and court decisions, are the same as in the case of other branches, and there may also be relevant international obligations binding on the country concerned. However, private international law differs from most other branches of national law, especially but not exclusively as regards the choice of law in labour matters, in the fact that there is comparatively little legislation or case law in this field. One result of this state of affairs is the importance, as a subsidiary source of law in this respect, of the views of writers and learned bodies; the question also arises whether collective agreements might not have a role to play.

LEGISLATION

Some 40 countries have legislation dealing specifically with private international law. Such legislation may be part of civil codes or take the form of special laws. In some cases the legislation is old; in others it is recent. Sometimes it is very detailed; elsewhere it may be limited to a few points.

In a minority of cases such legislation includes express provision on the law to be applied to labour relations with an international element. This is the case in Albania (article 20 of Act No. 3920 of 21 November 1964); [1] Austria (section 44 of federal Act of 15 June 1978); [2] Czechoslovakia (article 16 of Act No. 97 of 4 December 1963); [3] the German Democratic Republic (article 27 of Act determining applicable law of 5 December 1975); [4] Hungary (sections 51 to 53 of Legislative Decree No. 13 of 1979); [5] Kuwait (article 62 of Law No. 5 of 1961 on regulation of legal relations with a foreign element); [6] Poland (article 32 of Act concerning private international law of 12 November 1965); [7] and Spain (article 10(6) of the new preliminary provisions of the Civil Code, 1974).[8] Except in the case of Hungary, the express provisions on the subject consist of only one article.

5

The legislation of a number of other countries, although not dealing expressly with labour relations, contains provisions on the law applicable to contracts. The question then arises whether these provisions cover employment contracts. In Italy, courts have taken the view that article 25 of the preliminary provisions of the Civil Code, of 1942, does so apply, although some writers have questioned the appropriateness of this ruling.[9] The position in Argentina, regarding articles 1205 to 1210 of the Civil Code, may be similar.[10] In Greece also courts have applied article 25 of the Civil Code, on the law applicable to contractual relations, to labour matters.[11] On the other hand, in Brazil both the courts and commentators have considered article 9 of the introduction to the Civil Code to be inapplicable to labour relations.[12] Applicability to labour matters is likely to be related to the substance of the rule regarding contracts.[13]

Apart from provisions dealing specifically with labour relations or more generally with contracts, legislation on private international law frequently contains other provisions which have a bearing on the law governing employment. These provisions may deal with the law applicable to capacity to contract (relevant to the employment of minors); formalities to be observed (certain contracts of employment or particular provisions, such as those prohibiting competition, are often required to be in writing); and liability for injury or damage (this may relate both to damage caused by the worker and to claims by the worker outside the social security system). Of key importance are two types of general provision. One makes laws concerning public order and security applicable to all persons and events within the territory of the State enacting the provision;[14] "public order" is here given the sense of organisation of the State or the community.[15] The other reserves power to refuse to apply within that territory foreign law which runs counter to the fundamental principles accepted in the State concerned. Both will be considered in some detail later.

Statutes that are not specifically concerned with private international law may nevertheless contain provisions that affect the choice of law regarding a particular issue. In the main such provisions expressly define the scope of the legislation in which they are contained, extensively or restrictively. In recent years a practice has been developing of specifying in labour legislation that it applies to all contracts of employment for work within the country concerned, irrespective of the law which may otherwise govern the employment relation. That practice is followed in legal systems as diverse as those of Argentina,[16] Great Britain,[17] and a number of French-speaking African countries.[18] Special legislation on foreign investment,[19] on the employment of foreign specialists,[20] or on joint ventures [21] may also be of interest, in so far as it admits of variation of the law normally applicable to work within the country.

Finally, some account should be taken of legislation on private international law which exists in draft in a number of countries,[22] although in some cases it is unlikely to be adopted and in others it is probably some years away from being so. Three of these drafts (those of Argentina, Brazil and Switzerland) deal expressly with labour relations.

COURT DECISIONS

The role of the courts is to clarify the law in relation to actual situations and problems. In so doing, particularly on subjects concerning which there is little legislation, they may shape the law themselves. The formal authority of their decisions varies; thus, while in some countries the decisions of higher courts are binding on lower ones, this is not so elsewhere.

In any case if courts are to fulfil this role, disputes must be brought before them. The range of disputes that do come before the courts is affected by a number of factors. There is, first, their competence to consider disputes with a foreign element, and the extensive or restrictive interpretation given by them to that competence; this subject will be reviewed briefly in the next chapter. Secondly, there is the general pattern of dispute settlement in the country; some nations are more litigious than others and, more importantly in the labour field, there may be alternative, private forms of dispute settlement. Thirdly, the financial and other obstacles limiting access to courts are relevant; in that context the question whether a worker employed outside his own country can be represented by a union able and willing to support his claims is likely to be of importance. Finally, decisions on private international law presuppose that the court's attention has been drawn to the international aspects of the situation, although this may never occur if both parties are content to have a dispute decided on the basis of the local law.

Whatever the reasons may be, court decisions specifically concerned with international labour relations are not abundant anywhere.[23] There are sufficient decisions to make it possible to speak of patterns of case law in a number of Western European countries (Belgium, France, the Federal Republic of Germany, Italy and the Netherlands). In the United States there is ample case law concerning certain aspects of labour relations touching more than one of the constituent states of the federation; since these decisions touch on issues analogous to those of international relations, this case law is relevant. Judicial decisions in the United Kingdom relate mainly to the legislation referred to above. Elsewhere decisions are sparse.

In a survey of the law on the subject this paucity of case law creates a double danger: on the one hand too much importance may be attached to a decision dealing with a specific situation; on the other, isolated decisions may inadequately reflect the complexity of the relevant rules. These dangers are increased by two features of the case law. First, it will be seen from the next chapter that frequently the basis of a court's choice of law (whether it be the search for the implied or imputed intention of the parties or an objective rule in general terms such as the "closest connection" with the issue) leaves great discretion to the court to decide in the light of the circumstances of the particular case. Secondly it is widely recognised that there is a tendency to find a good reason for applying a law that is familiar.[24]

There is more case law on international contracts in general and on other issues of possible relevance to international labour relations, such as capacity, formalities or civil liability. As with respect to legislation, the applicability of the principles enunciated in these court decisions to the labour field cannot be taken for granted. But they do give precious indications on how related matters are handled.

TREATIES

Multilateral treaties covering large areas of private international law exist in Latin America. In particular 15 countries, including Brazil, Chile and Venezuela, are parties to the "Código Bustamante", adopted in 1928.[25] Two articles of the Code (197 and 198) deal with labour matters. The second of these articles, providing for the "territoriality" of protective labourlegislation, has coloured the approaches to international làbour relations in some of the countries concerned. The Montevideo Convention of 1940 on International Civil Law,[26] which is binding on Argentina, Paraguay and Uruguay, deals in article 28 with contracts for the rendering of services.

More specialised instruments on private international law, and in particular the treaties adopted at the various sessions of the Hague Conference on Private International Law, contain little of relevance to the present subject. However, the Convention on the Law Applicable to Contractual Obligations,[27] which became open for signature by States Members of the European Economic Community on 19 June 1980, deals specifically with contracts of employment. The Convention applies both to relations within the Community and to relations with parties outside. The Community is also considering the draft of a detailed regulation on conflicts of laws concerning labour relations within the Community.[28]

Amongst treaties which do not deal primarily with private international law but which determine the choice of law in particular substantive matters, mention must be made, first and foremost, of social security instruments. They exist at the international, regional, sub-regional and bilateral levels. Of international texts, three international labour Conventions are of importance: the Equality of Treatment (Accident Compensation) Convention, 1925 (Articles 1 and 2); the Equality of Treatment (Social Security) Convention, 1962; and, in particular, the Maintenance of Social Security Rights Convention, 1982 (Part II). Amongst European regional and sub-regional instruments reference should be made to the European Convention concerning the social security of international transport workers, 1956,[29] open to all European member States of the ILO (article 2); the European Convention on Social Security, 1972,[30] open to all member States of the Council of Europe (Title II); Regulation No. 1408/71 of the

European Economic Community,[31] (Title II); and the Agreement on the Social Security of Rhine Boatmen as revised in 1979 [32] (Title II). In Africa, the General Convention on Social Security of the African and Mauritian Common Organisation, of 1971 [33] (Title II), and the General Convention on Social Security of the Economic Community of the Countries of the Great Lakes, of 1978 (Title II), should be mentioned. In Latin America, the Andean Social Security Instrument of 1977 [34] is relevant. Bilateral conventions are too numerous to survey. However, account should be taken of the model clauses for such instruments attached to the Maintenance of Social Security Rights Recommendation, 1983.

Of instruments dealing with questions of employment and conditions of work, those relating to international transport are the most likely to contain provisions determining which law is applicable, expressly or by implication. Many international labour Conventions concerning maritime transport appear to imply such a determination, and this implication was confirmed by the ILO Committee of Experts on the Application of Conventions and Recommendations in 1957 with respect to the Seamen's Articles of Agreement Convention, 1926.[35] An express provision on the subject is contained in the European Agreement of 1970 concerning the work of crews of vehicles engaged in international road transport, concluded under the auspices of the United Nations Economic Commission for Europe.

Treaties concerning migrant workers, whether international (such as the international labour Conventions on migration for employment of 1949 and 1975), regional (such as the European Convention on the Legal Status of Migrant Workers of 1977), or bilateral, are more concerned with substantive standards of treatment than with determining the law to be applied to the migrants' employment relations. However, one question raised by them, which will be considered in Chapter III, is the extent to which a requirement that migrants be given treatment equal to that of nationals implies a choice of law. There are, moreover, some cases in which provision is made regarding the law governing employment relations: thus the Federal Republic of Germany includes a provision on the subject in model contracts attached to bilateral agreements regarding migration to its territory.[36]

The law applicable to employment relations tends to be dealt with also in three other kinds of international agreement which are rather specialised. One consists of treaties relating to persons regularly crossing frontiers for occupational purposes.[37] A second is that of agreements regarding major construction work astride national frontiers, such as the agreement between France and Spain regarding the bridge connecting Hendaye and Irun,[38] the arrangements between Argentina and Uruguay regarding the Salto Grande project,[39] those between Brazil and Paraguay regarding the Itaipú dam [40] and those between Argentina and Paraguay regarding work at Yaciretá.[41] Finally, there are agreements for co-operation on particular economic or technological projects, particularly amongst socialist countries.[42]

I

COMMENTATORS AND LEARNED BODIES

It is often alleged that there have been few publications on labour questions in connection with the study of private international law and few on problems of choice of law in connection with the study of labour law. The bibliography attached to this survey shows that its subject-matter does attract a certain interest. It also suggests, however, that most of the published work comes from a limited number of countries.

Where there is little positive law in the form of legislation, case law or international agreements, all that writers can do is to suggest appropriate solutions to problems in the light of the needs as they see them, the manner in which similar issues have been settled, and a basic philosophy of law. Unfortunately, these elements do not always lead to the same conclusions, and the value of the guidance to be derived from the views of individual authors is thereby diminished.

Rather more authority may attach to collective work. This is one reason for the relative importance of the draft legislation referred to above, even where it does not acquire force of law. Another example on the national plane is, in the United States, the second *Restatement of the Law* of the American Law Institute; [43] while in no way binding, it is widely taken into account in practice. Internationally, consideration has been given on two occasions in the past 30 years to the specific issue of conflicts of laws in labour matters: in 1957 the subject was on the agenda of the Second International Congress of Labour Law,[44] and in 1971 it was considered by the Institute of International Law, which embodied its conclusions in a resolution.[45]

COLLECTIVE AGREEMENTS

There are some collective agreements which lay down the law to be applied, generally to the employment of national workers sent abroad. These agreements differ from other sources used to determine the applicable law. First, they do not establish or suggest general rules of private international law, but seek to embody a particular body of law in specific employment relations; they are thus akin to the choice of law by the parties to the individual employment relation, to be considered in section A of the next chapter. Secondly, if their provisions diverge from the principles of private international law of the country concerned, their recognition, like that of a choice by the parties to an individual relation, depends on the admissibility of such a divergence. Thirdly, their applicability is itself dependent on a system of national law. The various problems regarding the position of collective agreements in private international law will be considered in Chapter IV.

Notes

[1] Text in A. N. Makarov: *Quellen des internationalen Privatrechts* (Tübingen, 3rd ed., 1978), "Nationale Kodifikationen".

[2] *Bundesgesetzblatt*, 1978, No. 109, p. 1729. See also E. Palmer in *Amer. J. Compar. Law*, 1980, pp. 197 ff.

[3] English text in *Bul. Czechoslovak Law*, 1963, Part 4, pp. 249 ff.

[4] *Gesetzblatt*, 1975, I, p. 748. See also an English version appended to F. K. Juenger: "The Conflicts Statute of the German Democratic Republic", in *Amer. J. Compar. Law*, 1977, p. 332.

[5] *Rev. crit.*, 1981, p. 171; summary by P. Szigeti in *Clunet*, 1980, pp. 636 ff.

[6] Text in Makarov: *Quellen des internationalen Privatrechts*, op. cit.

[7] Summary by D. Lasok in *Amer. J. Compar. Law*, 1966-1967, pp. 330 ff.

[8] Decree 1836/1974 of 31 May 1974. *Boletín Oficial del Estado*, 9 July 1974.

[9] Cassation, 3 Aug. 1968 (*Riv. dir. int. priv. proc.*, 1969, p. 777); Tribunal of Milan, inter alia, 11 May 1967 and 28 Feb. 1974 (ibid., 1968, p. 132 and 1976, p. 341); Tribunal of Trieste, 18 Mar. 1974 (ibid., 1975, p. 93); court of first instance of La Spezia, 4 Feb. 1977 (ibid., 1977, p. 876). For an analysis of commentaries see F. Pocar: "Le legge applicabile ai rapporti di lavoro secondo il diritto italiano", ibid., 1972, pp. 726-754. And see also G. Cian and A. Trabucchi: *Commentario breve al Codice Civile* (Padua, 1981).

[10] The amount of case law is not considerable, but for instance the Labour Court of Zarate on 9 Dec. 1970 applied article 1210 of the Civil Code to an employment contract concluded in Argentina for work in Venezuela (*Clunet*, 1972, p. 643). See also some older case law cited in W. Goldschmidt: "Derecho internacional privado del trabajo", in M. Deveali (ed.): *Tratado de derecho del trabajo*, Vol. IV (Buenos Aires, 1966). For a critical article see M. Deveali: "La relación de trabajo en el derecho internacional privado", in *Dº del trabajo*, 1952, p. 65.

[11] Decisions 421/1968 and 468/1969 of the Supreme Court, summarised in *Clunet*, 1971, pp. 331-335; decisions No. 5082 of 1972 and No. 558 of 1973 of the Court of Appeal of Athens, summarised ibid., 1976, pp. 963 ff.

[12] H. Valladão: *Direito internacional privado*, Vol. III (Rio de Janeiro, 1978), p. 99; A. Sussekind et al.: *Instituiçoes de direito do trabalho*, 6th ed., Vol. I (Rio, 1974), p. 131; G. M. C. Russomano: *Direito internacional privado do trabalho* (Rio, 2nd ed., 1979), p. 191.

[13] Other countries having legislation determining the law applicable to contracts that may cover contracts of employment are Algeria (article 18 of Civil Code, *Journal officiel*, 30 Sep. 1975); the Central African Republic (article 42 of Act No. 65-71 of 3 June 1975, in *Rev. crit.*, 1973, p. 394); Costa Rica (article 7 of Civil Code, in Makarov: *Quellen des internationalen Privatrechts*, op. cit.); Egypt (article 19 of Civil Code, in Makarov, op. cit.; it is there indicated that the Egyptian provision also served as a model for the civil codes of Iraq, the Libyan Arab Jamahiriya, Somalia and the Syrian Arab Republic); Gabon (article 55 of introductory part of Civil Code, in *Rev. crit.*, 1974, p. 844); Guatemala (article 24 of Aliens Act of 1936, in Makarov, op. cit.); Japan (sections 7 and 9 of "Horei" of 21 June 1898, in Makarov, op. cit.); Madagascar (article 30 of Ordinance No. 62-04, of 19 Sep. 1962, in *Rev. crit.*, 1964, p. 370); Nicaragua (article VI (14) of introductory provisions of Civil Code, in Makarov, op. cit.); Peru (article VII of introduction to Civil Code, in Makarov, op. cit.); Portugal (articles 41-42 of Civil Code, in *Rev. crit.*, 1968, p. 369); the Republic of Korea (article 9 of Act of 15 Jan. 1962 on private international law, in *Rev. crit.*, 1972, p. 347); Thailand (section 13 of Act of 10 Mar. 1938 on conflict of laws, in Makarov, op. cit.); and Uruguay (article 2399 of final provisions of Civil Code, in Makarov, op. cit.). The Fundamentals of Civil Legislation of the USSR, which contain provisions on contracts relating to foreign trade, do not apply to labour relations. The Fundamentals of Labour Legislation do not deal with private international law. However, the importance in Soviet private international law of article 12 of the Fundamentals of Civil Procedure ("In the absence of any law regulating a contested relation, the Court shall apply the law regulating analogous relations...") has been emphasised (see L. A. Lunz in *Rev. crit.*, 1964, p. 629).

[14] In addition to many of the countries listed in the preceding notes, Belgium, the Dominican Republic, France, Guinea, Haiti, Luxembourg, Mauritius and the Seychelles have legislative provisions on this point.

[15] See P. Francescakis in *Rev. crit.*, 1966, p. 13.

[16] Rules governing contracts of employment (*L.S.* 1976, Arg. 1), section 3.

[17] In particular the Employment Protection (Consolidation) Act, 1978, section 153 (5). For an analysis of all the British legislation in question and of case law relating thereto, see F. Gamillscheg: "Neue Entwicklungen im englischen und europäischen internationalen Arbeitsrecht", in *R.I.W./A.W.D.*, 1979, pp. 225-239.

[18] United Republic of Cameroon, Labour Code (*L.S.* 1974, Cam. 1), section 29; Gabon, Labour Code (*L.S.* 1978, Gab. 1), section 21; Ivory Coast, Labour Code (*L.S.* 1964, I.C. 1), section 29; Madagascar, Labour Code (*L.S.* 1975, Mad. 1), section 21; Mauritania, Labour Code (*L.S.* 1963, Mau. 1), section 6; Senegal, Labour Code (*L.S.* 1962, Sen. 2B), section 32.

[19] For instance Egyptian Act No. 43 of 1974 as amended by Act No. 32 of 1977 (English translation in *Yearbook of Federation of Egyptian Industries*, 1978, Legislative Acts, p. 47).

[20] For instance Brazilian Legislative Decree No. 691 of 18 July 1969, as cited in Machado, Piragibe and Malta, *Consolidação das leis do trabalho e legislação complementar*, 1º suplemento (Rio, 1969); and the relevant provisions of Romanian Aliens Law No. 25/1969 (*Clunet*, 1971, p. 541).

[21] For instance the Bulgarian law on joint ventures of 25 March 1980 (*Int. Legal Materials*, 1980, p. 992) and the regulations on labour management in joint ventures using Chinese and foreign investment, of 26 August 1980 (ibid., p. 1454).

[22] Argentina (draft code on private international law, 1964, in Makarov: *Quellen des internationalen Privatrechts*, op. cit.); Brazil (draft code of application of legal norms, 1970, ibid.); France (draft of 1967, in *Clunet*, 1971, p. 31); Switzerland (draft law on private international law, 1978, in *Etudes suisses de droit international*, Vol. 12 (Zurich, 1978); text submitted by the Government to Parliament on 10 November 1982, in *Feuille fédérale* (Berne), 1 Feb. 1983, pp. 255-501); Turkey (draft law on private international law and civil procedure, in *RabelsZ.*, 1982, pp. 26 ff.); Venezuela (draft of 1965, in Makarov, op. cit.).

[23] Published decisions are not necessarily an accurate reflection of those actually given. However, publications on the subject in different countries would make reference to unpublished decisions if they existed in significant numbers.

[24] F. Gamillscheg: "Intereuropäisches Arbeitsrecht", in *RabelsZ.*, 1973, pp. 284 ff. See also O. Kahn-Freund, "General problems of private international law", in *Cours Acad. droit int.*, 1974, III, at p. 426.

[25] Code of Private International Law, in Makarov: *Quellen des internationalen Privatrechts*, Vol. II (Tübingen, 2nd ed., 1960). Countries bound by the Code are Bolivia, Brazil, Chile, Costa Rica, Cuba, the Dominican Republic, Ecuador, Guatemala, Haiti, Honduras, Nicaragua, Panama, Peru, El Salvador and Venezuela.

[26] An English translation is given in Hudson: *International legislation*, Vol. 8: *1938-1941* (Washington, DC, 1949), pp. 513 ff. On its application to labour matters see Goldschmidt, op. cit. in note 10.

[27] *Official Journal of the European Communities*, L.266/1980. The Convention requires seven ratifications for entry into force. By spring 1983, the process of ratification was just beginning.

[28] Revised text submitted by the Commission to the Council in COM(75)653 final (28 Apr. 1976).

[29] *Official Bulletin* (Geneva, ILO), Vol. 39 (1956), No. 6.

[30] *European Treaty Series* (Council of Europe), No. 78, Jan. 1978.

[31] *Journal officiel des Communautés européennes*, L.149/1971.

[32] *Official Bulletin* (Geneva, ILO), Vol. 64 (1981), Series A, No. 1.

[33] *L.S.* 1971, Int. 1.

[34] Decision No. 113 of the Commission of the Cartagena Agreement. A Convention on social security adopted in 1967 by the Organisation of Central American States has not so far come into force.

[35] ILO: *Report of the Committee of Experts on the Application of Conventions and Recommendations*, Report III (Part IV), International Labour Conference, 40th Session, Geneva, 1957, p. 41.

[36] See, for instance, the agreements on recruitment and placement of Italian workers, of 16 April 1962 (*Bundesarbeitsblatt*, 1962, pp. 958-961); on temporary employment of Moroccan workers, of 21 May 1963 (ibid., 1963, pp. 602-603); and on recruitment and employment of Yugoslav workers, of 12 October 1968 (*Bundesgesetzblatt*, 1969, II, No. 33, pp. 1108-1113).

[37] Some examples are given in the *General report on conflict of laws in labour matters* to the Second International Congress of Labour Law (1957), pp. 41-42 and 150.

[38] *Journal officiel de la République française*, 27 July 1972.

[39] *D° del trabajo*, 1972, p. 479.

[40] See E. Córdova: "Labour law aspects of frontier works: The Itaipú Dam case", in *Int. Labour Rev.*, May-June 1976, pp. 303 ff.

[41] See E. L. Fermé: "Derecho internacional privado del trabajo", in Vasquez Vialard (ed.): *Tratado de derecho del trabajo*, Vol. II (Buenos Aires, 1982).

[42] See examples cited by the USSR in ILO: *Migrant workers*, Summary of reports on Conventions Nos. 97 and 143 and Recommendations Nos. 86 and 151, Report III (Part 2), International Labour Conference, 66th Session, 1980, at pp. 125-126.

[43] *Restatement of the Law 2nd*, "Conflict of Laws 2nd", adopted in May 1969 (St. Paul, Minnesota, 1971).

[44] On the results, see M. Simon-Depitre, in *Rev. crit.*, 1958, pp. 285 ff.

[45] *Ann. droit int.* (Basle), 1971, pp. 228-519.

PRINCIPLES OF PRIVATE INTERNATIONAL LAW GOVERNING THE INTERNATIONAL EMPLOYMENT RELATION

II

The present chapter reviews the chief questions that need to be settled in order to determine the legal framework of a particular international employment relation.

A. CHOICE OF LAW BY THE PARTIES TO THE INDIVIDUAL EMPLOYMENT RELATION

The individual employment relation is in the nature of a contract. Like contracts generally on the international as on the national plane, it reflects "shifting priorities between legislative ordering and private ordering".[1] In the private international law of contract, the main expression of "private ordering" is the choice of the law to be applied to the agreement by the parties themselves.

Contracts generally

As regards contracts generally, some scope for choice by the parties is given nearly everywhere.[2] Hesitation to allow for such choice has been most marked in Latin America, where national legislation on private international law does not provide for it, the Bustamante Code admits it only by implication, and the 1940 Additional Protocol to the Treaties on Private International Law of Montevideo[3] permits it only in so far as authorised by the law otherwise applicable (article 5). In practice, some room is left for private choice, and it is expressly contemplated in recent draft legislation. There nevertheless may be a difference of conceptual approach world-wide between the majority of countries, in which the decision of the parties is the primary basis for determining the law applicable to a contract with international elements, and a minority in which the main criteria for the determination are legislatively defined or otherwise "objective", the parties then being empowered, within limits to be considered below, to derogate from the main rule.

A requirement that the choice be express is rare.[5] In most countries it is accepted that a choice may also be implied. What may be meant by "implied" choice is described in the European Convention on the Law Applicable to Contractual Obligations as something "demonstrated with reasonable certainty by the terms of the contract or the circumstances of the case" (article 3, paragraph 1).[6] Elements widely regarded as constituting such demonstration are references to a particular system of law,[7] the use of a standard form of contract developed with a particular system of law in mind and, in some but not all countries,[8] the choice of the courts of a particular country for the settlement of disputes. In the absence of such "clear" manifestations of the actual will of the parties, recourse is had in some countries to the "objective" criteria to be discussed in section B below. In a number of countries, however, the search for a "hypothetical" or "imputed" party intention will be carried further, either before or in conjunction with such recourse, by weighing subjective considerations, such as the interest and convenience of the parties, to determine the law most appropriate to the relation. The case law is not very clear regarding the dividing line either between implied and imputed intention [9] or between subjective and objective criteria.

There are differences between countries concerning the time at which a choice of law may be made. In some, such as the Federal Republic of Germany, Poland and Switzerland, the choice may be made after the conclusion of the contract to which it relates and indeed as late as in the course of judicial proceedings concerning its application or interpretation (at which stage it is sometimes regarded as confirmation of an earlier choice); in those countries a modification of the original choice is also permitted.[10] The power of modification is also expressly provided for in article 3, paragraph 2, of the European Convention on the Law Applicable to Contractual Obligations. Other countries require the choice to be made at the time of the conclusion of the contract: for instance, this is expressly provided for by the Hungarian Legislative Decree of 1979 on Private International Law; it has also been the rule under Italian case law so far. Whatever the approach may be, it has been suggested that the parties can, in most countries, belatedly achieve the application of the law of the court seized of the dispute by abstaining from any reference to foreign contacts.[11]

There are also differences on the question whether the parties are free to choose any system of law whatsoever or whether their choice is limited to systems having some rational relation to the transaction at issue. The European Convention on the Law Applicable to Contractual Obligations places no general limits on the choice of the parties in this respect, and this fact probably corresponds to the existing practice of the countries that are members of the European Communities. The law and practice of an increasing number of other countries is similarly liberal. An express, general legislative limitation appears to exist at present in Gabon, where the choice must be made in pursuit of a "legitimate interest"; in Poland, where the choice must have some connection with the transaction at issue [12] and in Portugal, where the choice may only bear on a law the applicability of which corresponds to a "serious interest" or relates to one of the elements of the transaction taken into account by private international law. In the United States the second *Restatement of the Law*, in the volume on conflict of laws, makes a distinction: on an issue which the parties could have resolved by an explicit provision in their agreement, their choice of law is untrammelled; otherwise, their choice will not stand if the chosen law "has no substantial relationship to the parties or the transaction and there is no other reasonable basis for the parties' choice" (article 187). In some countries the requirement of a "reasonable interest" has been introduced for certain categories of contracts, as in the Federal Republic of Germany under the Act on Standardised Contractual Terms. More widely, reference has been made by courts and writers to a requirement of "good faith" [13] in the choice of law or, conversely, to an absence of fraudulent intent to evade the otherwise clearly applicable law. There is little guidance in practice on the circumstances in which a choice might be disregarded on this ground. Some writers consider that "good faith" is tantamount to "reasonable interest"; at the same time the notion of "reasonable interest" is very liberally interpreted. There is nevertheless one element of "good faith" to which specific reference should be made: it is widely held that a choice of foreign law is not permissible for an "internal" contract, i.e. one that involves no genuine foreign contacts; there have been affirmations that the establishment of foreign "addresses" for the sole purpose of creating a foreign contact would not be acceptable. Section 9 of the Hungarian legislative decree of 1979 expressly excludes a law made applicable by virtue of an artificially created foreign element.

A related question is whether the parties are bound to submit the contract in its entirety to one system of law, or whether they may make distinct elements of their transaction subject to different legal systems. The European Convention on Contractual Obligations expressly permits a choice of law for part of a contract; this apparently does not mean a multiplicity of choices, but rather a choice bearing on only one part, leaving the rest to be governed by the law otherwise applicable.[14] In the United States the choice contemplated in the second *Restatement of the Law*, in the volume on conflict of laws, is a determination issue by issue, and not for the transaction as a whole. Section 11 of the Czechoslovak Act of 1963 on Private International Law and Procedure makes it clear that the parties can choose different systems of law to govern the substance of the contract, on the one hand, and the consequences of its breach, on the other. However, case law, as a reflection of actual practice, is very sparse. Writers are divided on the admissibility of *dépeçage* – the "splitting up" of the contract. The main argument against allowing the parties to do as they wish in this respect is the need for a legal transaction to be governed by a single coherent system of rules. As will be seen from sections C and D below, this is in fact hardly ever entirely the case, because of other constraints on party choice.

Some problems arise also as regards the elements of the chosen law which become applicable. It is probably no longer maintained that, where a country distinguishes between public and private law, only the latter can apply.[15] There are nevertheless aspects of a legal system (for instance where the intervention of a public authority is required) which cannot readily be applied elsewhere on the basis of party choice. The question has also been raised whether the law chosen applies as it stands at the moment of choice, or whether subsequent changes become applicable. There is no unanimity on this point, either of commentators or of case law; revolutionary changes in legal systems and the effects of colonial accession to independence [16] have given rise to particular difficulties. Moreover, there is controversy on whether the law chosen becomes applicable to the contract in the manner in which it would be applied to an analogous agreement within the country of the law in question, or whether it is in fact adapted to the international relation. This has two aspects. First, there is the problem of *renvoi*: where the private international law of the chosen legal system would make the system of law of another country apply to a contract with the same features, does that other system become applicable? Legislation on private international law is very extensively based on the assumption that when the parties to a contract choose a system of law they have its ordinary substantive rules in mind, and that their choice accordingly excludes the possibility of subjection to another system.[17] Secondly, some elements of the chosen law may not apply to international contracts. The importance of this was made clear by a much criticised decision, in 1971, of the English Court of Appeal: a contractual clause (in a contract of employment) limiting liability for injury was found to be subject to the law of the Netherlands; it would not have been valid under English protective legislation and would apparently not have been valid under the law of the Netherlands either, had it been an "internal" contract, but the Court found that Netherlands law did not prohibit such clauses in "international" contracts.[18]

Finally, the effect of a choice of law by the parties may be circumscribed in two ways. On the one hand, elements of a legal system other than the one chosen may be made mandatorily applicable to the relationship. The legal system in question may be that which would have been applicable in the absence of party choice, that of the "forum", i.e. of a court considering an issue relating to the contract, or that of a third State having an important connection with the contract. The basis on which such legislation intervenes, including the question whether the choice of the parties prevails to the extent that it improves upon mandatory rules, will be considered in section C below. Conversely, the chosen law may be denied application by the State of the "forum" on the ground that its terms run counter to local "public policy"; this will be briefly discussed in section D. These two forms of state intervention, sometimes described as "positive and negative public policy", may very significantly reduce the effective scope of party choice as regards contracts affecting major economic or social concerns of States.

Contracts of employment are usually considered to be among the contracts in question.

Contracts of employment

A number of reasons are adduced by writers in favour of the view that a choice of law by the parties may be inappropriate for employment relations. There is, first, the consideration that the bargaining strength of the parties is not equal, particularly since contracts of employment are often in standard form, prepared by the employer, and there is thus no real joint choice. This argument, which was first advanced a long time ago,[19] has gained support in recent years as a consequence of the movement for the protection of consumers under standard contracts.[20] Secondly, emphasis is laid by some on the need for uniformity in the treatment of employees within the establishment at which they work.[21] This argument has been reinforced by reference to wider requirements of equality of treatment under treaties or national legislation.[22] Thirdly, employment relations are seen, over a wide spectrum ranging from the corporate to the welfare State, as a field in which the interest of the community in "legislative ordering" greatly outstrips the arguments in favour of "private ordering".[23]

These various arguments are contested. Thus it has been suggested that the first consideration is based on the fallacy that the law designated otherwise than by the choice of the parties will necessarily be more favourable to the "weaker party" than the law chosen by the parties.[24] To meet this objection, it is proposed [25] to give priority to whichever law (chosen or otherwise applicable) is the more favourable. The rub there, emphasised by the group which produced the Swiss draft on private international law,[26] is to determine what is more favourable (particularly if the determination is made for the relationship as a whole, and not issue by issue); also this solution runs counter to the second argument against party choice. A more circumscribed defence of party choice emphasises its usefulness for certain categories of employees such as managerial and technical staff who are regarded as able to look after themselves, and for certain types of detachment.[27]

Whatever may be the merits of the different arguments made on one side or another, there are treaties, legislation and case law which reflect, although in differing degrees, in differing ways and for differing reasons, the sentiment that contracts of employment are not altogether like other contracts.

It is rare at present for choice of law by the parties to be precluded altogether. Some writers consider that section 27 of the 1975 Act determining applicable law of the German Democratic Republic precludes it.[28] The official report on the Hungarian legislative decree of 1979 indicates that the decree does not allow the parties to an employment relation to choose the law governing it.[29] The draft regulation of the European Economic Community on conflicts of laws in employment relations, even in its more flexible 1976 version, would permit a choice of law by the parties only for limited categories of contracts of employment.[30]

In some countries the manner in which the choice is made, or the legal systems on which it bears, may be made subject to strict requirements in the case of contracts of employment. Thus the Austrian Act of 1978 on private international law, which permits implied as well as express choice of law by the parties for contracts generally, specifies in section 44 (3) that in the case of contracts of employment a contractual choice of law shall be taken into consideration only when it is made expressly. The Spanish decree of 1974 also requires express choice by the parties. The draft EEC regulation prescribes the systems of law between which the choice may be made for all categories of employees other than managerial, supervisory and technical staff.[31] Similarly, the Swiss Bill concerning private international law, as submitted to Parliament, permits a choice only of the law of the worker's ordinary place of residence or of that of the employer's place of business, domicile or ordinary residence. There are (possibly isolated) court decisions in the United States appearing to require a substantial relationship between the law chosen and the contract of employment,[32] and such a connection is required by article 32 of the Polish Act on private international law.

The question of the elements of the chosen law which become applicable raises some specific problems in the field of employment. First, there is the question of the applicability of national social security schemes. Because of the public and administrative nature of such schemes, it seems unlikely that a choice of law by the parties can of itself make such a scheme applicable where it bears on a system of law other than that (such as the law of the place of work) which would normally entail coverage. The strength of this consideration is confirmed, for instance, by a decision of the court of first instance of the City of Rome of 12 April 1977.[33] Further, to what extent does the law chosen for the individual employment relation embrace collective labour law? There is a trend of opinion, and some case law, in favour of the view that, in so far as collective agreements are part of the chosen law, they, or at least their provisions relating to individual employment relations, can become applicable.[34] The applicability of the provisions of that law regarding such matters as the conclusion of collective agreements, workers' representatives and workers' participation is much more open to question.[35] And there is no suggestion that the law regarding strikes is portable. These issues will be considered in more detail in Chapter IV.

In any case, the main means of circumscribing the effects of party choice in the field of employment is to make labour and social legislation of a legal system other than that chosen by the parties mandatorily applicable. As already indicated, this matter will be discussed in section C below. However, it is interesting to note that the more importance is given to such mandatory legislation, the more party choice comes to be seen as something that exists mainly for improving the protection afforded to workers. The

European Convention on the Law Applicable to Contractual Obligations provides in article 6, paragraph 1, that in a contract of employment a choice of law made by the parties shall not have the result of depriving the employee of the protection afforded him by the mandatory rules of the law which would be applicable in the absence of choice. It should be noted that, as explained in the report on the Convention by M. Giuliano and P. Lagarde,[36] collective agreements that have been made binding are regarded for purposes of the Convention as law the protection of which cannot be excluded by choice of law. The draft EEC regulation more specifically concerned with employment relations provides that, on a specified and wide range of subjects, party choice, even in the cases in which it is permitted, prevails only to the extent that it is more favourable to the employee (article 8, paragraph 3). The Austrian Act of 1978 on Private International Law provides that in a matter covered by mandatory provisions of the law applicable in the absence of choice, even an express choice of law must be disregarded if it was made to the detriment of the employee. Case law in Belgium,[37] Brazil [38] and France [39] tends in the same direction. So do the views of Scandinavian writers, in the absence of relevant case law.[40] Whether the law mandatorily applicable can in fact always be improved upon will be considered in section C.

At the same time, the importance of these tendencies, world-wide, must not be overestimated. Countries such as Australia, Canada, England and the Federal Republic of Germany,[41] which have been the bastions of freedom of the parties, do not at present recognise any need for limitations of principle of the freedom, although they do have legislation which in certain respects limits the effects of choice. Some legislation on private international law (that of Albania and Czechoslovakia) expressly provides for the possibility of choice of the law applicable to the employment relation by the parties, apparently without special limitation. Some special legislation on joint ventures, such as a Bulgarian law of March 1980 and the Chinese Regulations of August 1980 on Labour Management in Joint Ventures, provides for the labour relations of foreign workers to be governed essentially by the contract of employment. In Italy case law is at present more favourable to freedom of choice by the parties to contracts of employment than previously.[42] In other countries, such as Greece, the principles regarding party choice applicable to contracts generally appear to apply without reservations. In this respect as in other aspects of the subject to be considered later, there are national differences not only in positive law but in approaches to the policy options underlying the law.

B. THE LAW APPLICABLE TO THE EMPLOYMENT RELATION IN THE ABSENCE OF PARTY CHOICE

The systems of law ·to be considered as applicable in the absence of party choice are those which have some connection with the issue or the parties involved. Major "connecting factors" or "points of contact" are, as regards a contract, the place of conclusion or the place of performance and, as regards the parties, their respective or common nationality or residence, or, in the case of companies, the principal or a subsidiary place of business. The identification of some of these connecting factors is not self-evident: for instance, a contract may call for performance by both parties, in different places. Refinements have accordingly been developed, such as the (originally Swiss) notion of "characteristic performance", i.e. the essential feature of the type of contract in question.

There is no international consensus on the importance to be attached to different connecting factors. (There may be more convergence on the practical effect of the solutions adopted than on the grounds for their adoption.) There is, in particular, a fundamental difference between countries in which a particular factor must be strictly applied, often under legislation, and countries in which each case is determined in accordance with flexible criteria that can be adapted to the circumstances. Among such criteria particular mention should be made of the notion of the "proper law" of the issue, used in many countries of the Commonwealth and by Greece, and the notion of the *Schwerpunkt*, the "centre of gravity" of the relation, used in the Federal Republic of Germany; both involve a search for the closest contact between a system of law and the matter at issue.

As regards employment relations, some distinction must be made here between the "typical" arrangement, under which the employee works in one fixed place for the entire period of employment (and which is the situation of most migrant workers) and special cases such as those of temporary or permanent detachment or transfer, work in more than one place, and work not linked to any fixed place.

The "typical" employment relation

A number of enactments on private international law attach a certain importance, as regards contracts in general, to the place of conclusion.[43] It is considered by some authorities that this test is inappropriate to the employment relation. It was for this reason, for instance, that courts and writers have been at one in Brazil to regard article 9 of the introduction to the Civil Code, under which the place of conclusion is the main connecting factor, as being inapplicable to contracts of employment.[44] Certainly not a single legislative provision at present in force and specifically concerned with the law applicable to labour relations uses this connecting factor, even subsidiarily. The main arguments that have been made against it are that the place of conclusion is often fortuitous, that in the case of standard contracts little significance attaches to their "conclusion", and that practical difficulties arise if the parties were not in the same place at the time of conclusion since different systems of law embody different notions concerning the place of conclusion of the contract in such a case.[45] However, not all practice is as clear-cut as that. Italian courts have on a number of occasions used the place of conclusion, which under article 25 of the preliminary provisions of the Civil Code is one of the connecting factors subsidiary to party choice, to determine the law applicable to an employment relation; in some of the cases in question, but by no means all, this practice has led to the application of Italian law.[46] Moreover, there have been cases in which courts enjoying greater discretion in the choice of connecting factor have taken the place of conclusion, not necessarily on its own, into consideration in the determination of the law applicable to employment relations; this has been the case, for instance, in Belgium.[47] In a recent decision of the English Court of Appeal concerning the law applicable to a collective agreement concluded on behalf of the International Transport Workers' Federation with the agent of the owners of a ship flying a flag of convenience, the fact that the agreement was concluded in Spain, where the owners hoped to recruit their crews, was regarded as a major element pointing to the applicability of Spanish law.[48] For a worker recruited at his home for work elsewhere, the place of conclusion of the contract may represent the system of law with which he is most familiar and in which he has most confidence. There will also be cases in which that law is more favourable to the worker than that of the place at which the work is performed; accordingly as regards contracts of employment the 1974 Argentine draft of a code on private international law provides that as between the law of the place of conclusion and that of the place of performance, the court shall choose that which is more favourable for the worker. On the other hand recourse to the law of the place of conclusion of individual contracts takes no account of such considerations as the desirability of uniform treatment of employees within the establishment at which they work.

The common nationality or the common domicil or residence of the parties may also represent a system of law known to them, and in which they have confidence. Again under some legislative provisions regarding the law applicable to contracts generally these are regarded as connecting factors,[49] often in preference to the place of conclusion. Of the legislation specifically concerned with employment relations, that of Poland gives primary importance, after party choice, to the law of the country in which both parties reside or do business at the time they contract. Both in countries with legislation on the subject and in those where in general terms a close relation is required between a contract and the law to be applied thereto, this test has been used by the courts for employment relations. This is so, for instance, in Belgium (where the combination of that factor and that of the place of conclusion tends to override other considerations); [50] France; [51] the Federal Republic of Germany (where the Federal Labour Court has stated that "the fact that both parties have the same nationality is accepted as presumptive evidence of their having chosen the law of their home country" and held that in particular cases it may outweigh the importance of the place where the employee normally does his work); [52] and Italy.[53]

Recourse to common nationality or domicil as a connecting factor is not open to certain of the objections made to use of the place of conclusion of the contract. At the same time, this test cannot serve either to achieve unified treatment of persons working in the same establishment.

The employer's principal place of business is not widely regarded as a major connecting factor for the "typical" employment relation, although it acquires key importance in some of the special cases to be considered below. It is used nevertheless in several provisions on the law applicable to employment relations in general. The Czechoslovak Act of 1963 on international civil law provides that where an employee works in one country under a contract of employment with an undertaking having its head office in another country, the location of the head office shall be the determining factor unless the worker is domiciled in the country where he works. Similarly the 1975 Act determining applicable law, of the German Democratic Republic, provides that employment relations are governed by the law of the State of the employer's principal place of business, except where the place of work is situated in the State of the employee's habitual residence. The Kuwait Act of 1961 on regulation of legal relations with a foreign element provides that the law applicable to contracts of industrial, commercial and agricultural undertakings with their workers shall be that of the area from which the undertaking is run; at the same time, if the registered office is abroad but the contract was concluded by a branch of the undertaking in Kuwait, Kuwait law applies. The Polish Act of 1965 refers to the law of the head office of the undertaking for cases in which the employee works on its premises. There have, moreover, been judicial decisions which have recognised that in certain employment, even though the employees may not be required to travel, the registered office of the employing undertaking is the main point of contact and unifying element. It was for these reasons that in 1971 the English Court of Appeal found the law of the Netherlands to be the "proper law" of an employment relation under which an English employee worked offshore in Nigerian waters for the Netherlands subsidiary of a United States corporation.[54] The report on the EEC Convention on the Law Applicable to Contractual Obligations also suggests that the law of the registered head office of the employing undertaking should be applied to employment offshore. This point will be considered further below.

However, it is the law of the place where the work is performed which is generally considered to be the most appropriate for the majority of "typical" employment relations. Normally, it is the place where the employee is integrated into a working community. Recourse to its law then permits both the equal treatment of employees working together and the operation of a coherent system of rules, because the application of certain elements of that law is likely to be mandatory, as will be seen from the next section.

International instruments dealing with the law applicable to employment relations invariably give preference to this connecting factor. The Montevideo Convention of 1940 on International Civil Law provides in article 38, as regards contracts for services, that if their effect is linked to a particular place the law of that place applies; this provision is interpreted as referring primarily to the place where the work is performed.[55] The EEC Convention on the Law Applicable to Contractual Obligations makes the law of the country in which the worker habitually carries out his work applicable in the absence of party choice.[56] The draft EEC regulation on conflicts of laws in employment relations would use a similar test (except that, as indicated above, it would in many cases make it applicable to the exclusion of party choice). International and regional or sub-regional social security conventions, other than those concerned with transport workers, use the place where the work is carried out as the main connecting factor for determining what law is applicable.

With the exception of that of Kuwait, all legislation specifically concerned with the law applicable to the employment relation makes some use of this test. The Albanian Act of 1964 concerning the civil rights of aliens and the application of foreign law provides that if not otherwise agreed, contracts of employment shall be subject to the law of the country in which the work is performed. The Austrian Act of 1978 makes the main test for contracts of employment the law of the country in which the employee habitually carries out his work. The Czechoslovak Act of 1963 provides that unless agreed otherwise contracts of employment shall be governed by the law of the country in which the worker performs his work: it makes an exception, as indicated above, for cases in which the head office of the employing undertaking is in a different country, but maintains the main rule even in such a case if the employee's domicil is in the country in which he performs his work. In the German Democratic Republic reference to the place of work is subsidiary to a main rule based on the employer's principal place of business; it applies if the place of work is located in the State of the employee's habitual residence. In practice the law of Czechoslovakia and of the German Democratic Republic must have analogous results, i.e. to apply the law of the place of performance if that place is also either the employer's principal place of business or the employee's habitual place of residence. On the other hand the Hungarian law of 1979, like those of Albania and Austria, makes the law of the country in the territory of which the work is performed the sole test for the typical employment relation. That is also the situation under Spanish law. In Poland, where, as indicated above, prime importance is attached to the common residence of the parties, the country in which the work is to be performed is the test for cases in which the parties do not reside or maintain a place of business in the same country. One might add that, where legislative provisions applicable to contracts in general attach prime importance to the place of performance, as do articles 1209 and 1210 of the Argentine Civil Code (except with respect to contracts concluded abroad for performance abroad), they can be applied in respect of contracts of employment as referring to the place at which the employee carries out his work.[57]

Case law shows some divergent trends. First, in countries such as Italy in which the courts accept the relevance to contracts of employment of general legislative provisions on the law applicable to contracts, and in which those provisions call for the use of rigidly defined connecting factors which do not include the place of performance, little importance is attached, as regards the law applicable to employment relations, to the place where the work is carried out. Secondly, there are countries in which case law has given key importance to that place. This is true of Brazil, at any rate as regards work performed in Brazil, and of the Netherlands, where the Supreme Court, in a decision of 8 June 1973, stated it to be a rule of the country's private international law regarding contracts of employment that if, in the absence of a choice of law, a specific country could be indicated as the place where the work in question was normally performed, it was the law of that country which governed the contract.[58] Thirdly, in a number of countries courts enjoying sufficiently wide discretion in the matter consider the place at which the work is carried out to be a major, but not necessarily controlling, indicator of the law having the closest relation with the employment contract. This is so, for instance, in Belgium,[59] France [60] and the Federal Republic of Germany.[61]

It might finally be mentioned that the Swiss Bill on private international law, as submitted to Parliament, would apply to contracts of employment the law of the country in which the employee habitually carries out his work; that in the United States the second *Restatement of the Law*, in its volume on conflict of laws, provides for the applicability of the law of the state where the contract requires that the services, or a major portion of the services, shall be rendered; and that the Institute of International Law, in its resolution of 1971, made the law of the country in which the work is to be performed applicable.

From the foregoing, it would be legitimate to conclude that in the absence of a choice of law by the parties the place at which the work is performed is widely though not universally recognised to be the most appropriate connecting factor for determining the law applicable to the typical employment relation, but that it is also widely felt that use of that factor may not be suitable in every such relation. It is for the latter reason that reference to that factor in recent texts tends to be accompanied by escape clauses. The EEC Convention on the Law Applicable to Contractual Obligations makes the main principle inapplicable if "it appears from the circumstances as a whole that the contract is more closely connected with another country". The Swiss Bill, as submitted to Parliament, provides, more generally, that the law which is normally applicable shall exceptionally not be applied where there is clearly a much closer link with another system of law. The United States *Restatement* makes the main rule on contracts for the rendition of services inapplicable where "with respect to the particular issue, some other State has a more significant relationship ... to the transaction and the parties". In its decision of 1973 cited above, the

Supreme Court of the Netherlands made the rule enunciated subject to the proviso that there may be special circumstances as a consequence of which the contract of employment ought to be governed by the law of a different country. Safeguards of this kind, like the circumspection of some case law, ensure a flexibility which may be desirable in the interests of justice. They do not make it easy for the parties and others concerned to foresee with certainty what the law governing their relationship will be.

Special situations

Temporary detachment

It appears to be generally accepted that an employee who is temporarily sent abroad by the employing undertaking remains subject to the law previously applicable. The EEC Convention on the Law Applicable to Contractual Obligations, which normally applies to contracts of employment the law of the place where the worker "habitually" carries out his work, adds expressly that the rule is not affected by the temporary detachment of the worker to another country. Regional and sub-regional social security conventions establish a similar principle (which may there be of particular importance for the maintenance of rights). The widely accepted German theory of *Ausstrahlung* (the extension of the law of the ordinary place of work or, as it is sometimes expressed, the extended influence of the place of business of the undertaking at which the worker is normally employed) embraces the situation of temporary assignment abroad. According to Professor Szaszy,[62] legislation such as that of Czechoslovakia, according to which the law of the head office of the undertaking is applicable to employees working in another country, is intended to cover such assignments. The Austrian law of 1978 specifies that the State in which the employee usually carries out his work remains the determining factor if the employee is sent to a place of work in another State. In Great Britain, the definition of the scope of labour legislation by reference to "ordinary work" in or outside the country achieves a similar result. Case law is not plentiful, but in a decision of 29 July 1974 [63] the Italian Court of Cassation regarded as subject to Italian social security legislation a worker sent to Spain by his Italian employer for the limited purpose of erecting a crane.

There is a tendency to assimilate special recruitment for short-term service abroad to temporary detachment. This is true mainly of the operation of temporary work agencies across frontiers; [64] there have been other cases in which some elements of the law of the country of origin have been applied to a contract of employment specifically concluded for a short mission abroad.[65]

What is not altogether clear is the period to be regarded as "temporary". Social security conventions make the test either six months or one year, generally with a possibility of extension.[66] There is no express definition elsewhere; indeed the draft EEC regulation on conflicts of laws in employment relations merely refers to the definition given in Community social security provisions. It may be that a flexibly interpreted period of one year would correspond to most widely held conceptions. However, in practice the issue is blurred by the fact that in some cases employees detached for much longer periods may remain subject to the former law.

Long-term detachment or transfer

It is widely considered, as a basic rule, that but for the possibility of party choice to the contrary,[67] employees detached or transferred to another country for an indefinite period of time become subject to the law of the new place of performance.[68] Indeed such a rule would seem to be implied by the limitation in time of the rules regarding temporary detachments. Some case law confirms this assumption.[69]

However, this type of detachment or transfer concerns, above all, the managerial and technical staff of undertakings with operations abroad and, in particular, of groups of companies. For a variety of reasons, which can be described collectively as continued links with a home base, it has seemed appropriate in many of the cases of such detachment or transfer that the law of the original base should continue to apply even in the absence of party choice to that effect. A very substantial part of the case law on the whole subject of conflicts of laws in labour matters is concerned with these situations. Belgian courts have attached importance, in that connection, to the fact that the authority of the employer has been continuously exercised from the "home" country.[70] The view taken by courts in France and the Netherlands is analogous.[71] In the Federal Republic of Germany the concept of *Entsendung* covers the group of employees in question, who are considered to remain subject to the law of the place from which they are sent.[72] In Great Britain, where the question has arisen in terms of the applicability of local legislation, a kind of "base" test has also been evolved.[73] In the case of groups of companies, such detachments also raise the question as to who is the real employer: that point will be considered in Chapter III.

Work in several countries concurrently

The problem of a "base" arises also where the employee does not perform his work in one country alone. This may be the case for certain types of managerial or specialist staff, who move in an advisory capacity from country to country; it may be the case of some commercial representatives, though by no means all; it is also the case of workers in road, rail and air transport and inland navigation. The connecting factor generally used for these situations is that of the location of the employing undertaking: this may be taken to be the undertaking's principal place of business, but also the location of the particular branch or establishment employing and supervising the worker. For air transport and inland navigation preference is given by some to the place of registration of the aircraft or vessel.

A number of international treaties deal expressly with the employment relations in question. The EEC Convention on the Law Applicable to Contractual Obligations specifies that in cases in which the employee does not habitually carry out his work in any one country, the contract of employment shall be governed (subject to the usual escape clause) by the law of the country in which the place of business through which he was engaged is situated. The draft EEC regulation does not lay down a firm rule for these cases, but leaves it to the parties to choose between the law of one of the countries in which the worker carries out his work, the law of the country in which the worker has his permanent residence, and the law of the country in which the employer is domiciled or the establishment has its registered office. In respect of matters dealt with in the 1970 European Agreement concerning the work of crews of vehicles engaged in international road transport (manning, driving periods and rest periods), the Agreement requires compliance with the law of the country in which the driver normally carries out his work. The various regional and sub-regional social security conventions all provide, in this context, for the applicability of the law of the registered office of the employing undertaking; [74] in the two Conventions concerned with transport workers (the 1956 European Convention concerning the social security of international transport workers, and the Agreement on the social security of Rhine boatmen as revised in 1979), this is the main rule. Finally, the test of the Montevideo Convention of 1940, regarding an effective link between the contract and a particular place, has apparently been so interpreted as to permit recourse to the law of the place of the registered office of the employing undertaking where it constitutes the constant base. [75]

National legislation also frequently makes special provision for all or some of the cases in question. The Albanian law of 1964 makes the law of the place where the employing undertaking is located applicable to road and rail transport. The Austrian Act of 1978 provides that if the employee usually carries out his work in more than one State or if he has no habitual place of work, the law of the State in which the employer has his habitual residence or his permanent business establishment shall prevail. The Czechoslovak law of 1963 provides that the contracts of employment of transport workers shall be governed, in the case of rail and road transport, by the law of the country of the principal place of business of the undertaking concerned, and, in the case of inland waterways and air transport, by that of the place of registration. It should be recalled that in the German Democratic Republic, where there is no special provision on the subject, applicability of the law of the country of the employer's principal place of business is the prevailing rule for all contracts of employment. The Hungarian law of 1979 makes the law to which the employer is subject applicable to employment spanning several countries, and to road and rail transport. The Swiss Bill submitted to Parliament is similar to the Austrian Act.

Case law is not plentiful. Reference should, however, be made to the decision of the Supreme Court of the Netherlands of 8 June 1973,[76] in which it indicated, in the course of a statement of the private international law of the Netherlands on contracts of employment, that where an employee's field of operations extends over more than one country the contract of employment should be governed by the law of the country where the employee is normally stationed pursuant to his contract or, if no such country can be indicated, by the law of the country where the employer is established. In its decision of 10 April 1975, referred to earlier,[77] the Federal Labour Court of the Federal Republic of Germany did not establish any general rule, but it did apply the law of the registered office of the employing undertaking to the contract of an airline pilot, partly on the ground that the pilot did not work in a single place.

· Work for an undertaking astride a frontier is rather an unusual variant of the situation dealt with under this heading. Some of the regional social security instruments deal with it and make the law of the country in which the employing undertaking has its principal place of business applicable. This solution does not necessarily correspond to that agreed for specific construction operations. Thus, for workers employed in the river bed of the Salto Grande project between Argentina and Uruguay, the law, including the collective agreements, of the country in which the contract was concluded (and in which the worker is perhaps likely to have had his normal residence) was made applicable.

Seafarers

Work in maritime shipping differs from the typical employment situation in that seafarers are constantly on the move. It differs from other cases of moving workers both in that there is a "fixed" place of work (the vessel) which is regarded under public international law as part of the territory of the State whose flag it flies, and in that, for a substantial proportion of time, the place of work moves across areas not owned by any State.

The traditional solution has been, and largely remains, the application of the law which corresponds most closely to that of the place of performance on land, namely the law of the flag. European social security instruments use this as the main rule for employment at sea. Most international labour Conventions regarding maritime employment require that they be applied by the State of registration of the vessel, a test which generally corresponds to that of the flag. The interpretation placed on one of them, the Seamen's Articles of Agreement Convention, 1926, by the ILO Committee of Experts on the Application of Conventions and Recommendations is that the terms of maritime employment contracts should be subject to the law of the State of registration.[78] The legislation of Albania, Czechoslovakia and Hungary on private international law expressly makes the law of the flag applicable to maritime employment. So do a number of national maritime codes, regarding service on ships flying their flag.[79] There is also case law establishing this basic rule.[80]

However, as in the case of the law of the place of performance, it is being increasingly recognised that there may be circumstances in which the main rule is unsuitable. There appear to be three grounds, in practice, for diminishing its authority.

The first, and most limited in scope, relates to employment which in fact is carried out entirely within the waters of one State. The European social security instruments provide that where work is performed on a vessel in the territorial waters or ports of a particular State by persons not members of the crew of the vessel, the law of that State applies. Somewhat more widely the Argentine National Labour Appeals Court held, on 14 September 1970,[81] that the law of the flag was not applicable to coastal trade in national waters, and applied Argentine law to the contracts of seafarers hired in Argentina and employed on a Panamanian vessel exclusively in Argentine waters; it should be noted that the contracts expressly accepted the jurisdiction of Argentine courts and that the crew was covered by Argentine social security.

Secondly there are cases in which a seafarer has a continuing contract with a shipping firm in one country, this being expressly envisaged as one of the means of ensuring continuity of employment in the ILO's Continuity of Employment (Seafarers) Convention, 1976, but is assigned for service on a vessel flying a different flag. The European social security instruments treat this like other cases of detachment, and provide for the continuing applicability of the original law. There appears to be little authority on whether the same is true regarding the law applicable to the employment relation in general, but there may be good reasons, such as preservation of various entitlements, for an affirmative answer. In one decision, of 17 September 1974, the Federal Labour Court of the Federal Republic of Germany held that while detached to ships sailing under a foreign flag, ships' officers with a continuing contract with a shipping firm of the Federal Republic were covered by the Works Constitution Act in relation to the firm.[82]

Thirdly and perhaps most importantly, there is the problem of flags of convenience.[83] One argument made against the law of the flag in such cases, namely that the flag State cannot always enforce its law, is not necessarily conclusive; although a relation between the two may be desirable, enforcement of mandatory law, on the one hand, and the law governing the employment relation, on the other, are distinct issues. A more telling objection to the law of the flag in such cases may be that it has no genuine connection with either party to the contract of employment. There is accordingly a tendency to have recourse to other points of contact, i.e. to look for the "proper law" of the relationship. The European social security instruments provide that where the seafarer is paid by an undertaking having its principal place of business in a country other than that of the flag and he himself resides in that country, its law shall apply. The British Merchant Shipping Act, 1970, allows the principle of the "proper law" to operate in relation to contracts of maritime employment; [84] it also provides for the maintenance of certain rights in the event of a change in the registration of a vessel. Section 87 of the Finnish Seamen's Act, 1978, empowers the Government to prescribe that the Act applies to an employment relation on board a foreign vessel between a Finnish employer and a Finnish seafarer. There is also case law in which the veil of the flag has been moved aside to reveal the principal place of business of the owner. For instance in Brazil the Regional Labour Court of Rio de Janeiro on 25 October 1948 decided not to apply the law of the (Panamanian) flag in a case in which the owner of the vessel was domiciled in Brazil and wages were paid in Brazilian currency.[85] In Greece, also, courts early decided to determine the "proper law" of contracts of maritime employment case by case; while they often attached importance to the nationality of the seafarer, or the place of conclusion of the contract, it has been suggested that an unavowed determining factor was the beneficial ownership of the shipping company.[86] In the United States the Supreme Court on 8 June 1970, admittedly for the limited purpose of the application of United States legislation on injuries to seafarers, abandoned its usual deference to the law of the (Greek) flag by reference to the United States domicil of the owner of the ship.[87] In the Federal Republic of Germany also, a regional labour court on 17 July 1980 applied the law of the Federal Republic to the relation between two of its nationals, namely a shipowner and an employee, on a ship flying the Cyprus flag.[88]

Employment on fixed offshore installations

Floating structures which cannot be said to be ships are nevertheless widely assimilated to ships in so far as they are on the move.[89] Whether this is necessarily appropriate for all categories of persons employed on them may be arguable, but the assimilation provides a basic rule of reference. There is no such rule for fixed offshore installations. Reference has been made above, under the "typical" employment relation, to views that the connecting factors usually applicable to that relation require adaptation in the case of work offshore. There are two reasons for such a need: many of the installations in question are not in the territory of any State; and, even where they are in territorial waters of a State, the owner of the installation and some or all of the persons employed on it may have no other relation with the State concerned.

Consideration of the employment aspects of offshore operations has so far been largely focused on the applicability or otherwise of protective legislation, on the basis of the extension of jurisdiction to the continental shelf, or the exercise of jurisdiction over installations by virtue of their registration or over persons by virtue of their nationality or domicil. Little thought appears to have been given to the distinct question of the law governing employment relations,[90] perhaps because the practice of some of the major countries concerned by offshore activities is in any case not tied to rigid connecting factors. As has been seen above, such comments as there have been on the subject (in the report on the EEC Convention on the Law Applicable to Contractual Obligations, and in the view at least of the majority of the English Court of Appeal in the *Sayers* case) have considered the law of the employer's principal place of business to be the most appropriate. It would have the advantage of implying uniform treatment of the workforce, as would the possible alternative of the law of the place of registration of the installation. It is, however, open to question whether either adequately meets all situations. For instance, where a national of the United Kingdom who is domiciled in that country leaves it for tours of duty on a rig under United States ownership which is installed on the British continental shelf, there may be much to be said for the application of the law of the domicil or the "base" of the employee.[91] Moreover, since some of the legislation on offshore exploration has made it a condition of a licence, for tax reasons, that the prospector be incorporated in the country granting the licence, his place of business may not correspond to real ownership. This would accordingly seem to be a field in which there is a need, at this stage, to leave the "proper law" to be determined in each case. Reasonable certainty can then be achieved, within the limits of mandatorily applicable law, only by the express choice of the parties.

C. LEGAL PROVISIONS OVERRIDING THE LAW OTHERWISE APPLICABLE

Whether the law governing the employment relation is determined by the choice of the parties or by reference to the principles examined in the preceding section, some aspects of that relation are likely to be regulated by legal provisions which are not part of the legal system so determined. Such provisions are largely, but not necessarily, elements of the law at the place where the work is performed. The question of their application arises differently according to whether they are part of the "law of the forum" (i.e. of the State in which an issue regarding the employment relation is being settled) or not.

The law of the State of the forum

As regards the law of the State of the forum, what happens is that certain provisions of the substantive law of the State concerned are applied both instead of the general rules of private international law of that State [92] and in spite of the fact that the parties favour another legal system. The specific reasons for such an occurrence differ. Indeed, where there is no party choice and the State of the forum is also that in which the work is performed (or, as the case may be, in which the undertaking has its registered office), it is not always easy to be certain that particular rules are applied as an exception to, and not as part of, the law applicable under the State's own general rules of private international law.

The most straightforward situation is that of enactments which, by their express terms, require to be applied to the exclusion of any other law. Thus the Argentine rules governing contracts of employment [93] provide that they apply to all matters relating to the legal capacity, rights and obligations of the parties, regardless of whether the contract of employment was concluded in Argentina or abroad, on condition that it is performed in Argentina. The labour codes of a number of predominantly French-speaking African States [94] specify that every contract of employment concluded for performance within the country is subject to their terms, irrespective of where it is concluded and where either of the parties resides. This is true even of partial performance within the country of a contract concluded under foreign law; only temporary missions for less than three months are excluded. In Great Britain major legislation in the field of employment – the Employment Protection (Consolidation) Act, 1978 (section 153 (5)), the Equal Pay Act, 1970 (section 1 (11)), and the Trade Union and Labour Relations Act, 1974 (section 30 (b)) – expressly declares the law of the employment relation to be irrelevant to the scope of application of that legislation. Unlike that of the preceding examples, the scope of the British legislation is linked not so much to performance of the work within the country as to the fact that the employees concerned "ordinarily" work there; court decisions imply that work carried out within the country for quite substantial periods may not be covered, while not all work abroad makes the legislation inapplicable.

The labour legislation of certain other countries specifies that it applies to all work performed within the country and that its applicability shall not be excluded by private agreement. For instance, the Labour Code of Ecuador [95] provides that contracts of employment shall be governed by the provisions of the Code even if they do not expressly refer to it and notwithstanding any stipulation to the contrary. It is not always easy to be sure, in the absence of a specific indication, that such provisions apply to international as well as internal employment contracts. The federal Act of 1980 to regulate employment relationships of the United Arab Emirates [96] makes this perhaps somewhat clearer by specifying that non- nationals may not perform work within the country otherwise than subject to the conditions specified in the Act, while the General Labour Law of Angola [97] states that it applies to foreign citizens recruited for work in Angola. Similarly, the Labour Code of Iraq [98] provides that it shall apply to every worker within the country.

In some countries the conclusion has been drawn, in particular from the protective nature of labour law, that it must apply in its entirety to work performed within the country concerned. This interpretation has been placed, in particular, on article 198 of the Código Bustamante to the effect that legislation for the social protection of workers is territorial. In Brazil, the provision of article 444 of the Consolidated Labour Laws to the effect that the parties may not exclude or contravene protective legislation or applicable collective agreements has been considered to apply to international employment relations involving work in Brazil.[99] Perhaps for analogous reasons and with analogous results, the federal Labour Act of Mexico [100] and the Labour Code of Panama [101] are declared to be *de orden publico*. Again, it is difficult to know whether references to "public policy" are only of internal importance or cover "international public policy", i.e. policy concerns of relevance in international relations. The Panamanian Code clarifies this by adding (section 2) that its terms are binding on all persons and undertakings in Panamanian territory.

In a considerable number of countries with some legislation on private international law it is provided that "laws concerning public order and security" shall be compulsorily binding on all persons within the territory of the country concerned. Elsewhere, public policy has been invoked in order, similarly, to establish the imperative character of particular legal provisions. There is a substantial body of published work on what this may mean in terms of state intervention in economic and social matters affecting labour in particular.[102] There is also case law with specific bearing on labour matters, largely as regards dismissals.

In the light of legislation specifically made applicable, and of writings and case law regarding more general provisions, it is possible to determine the main categories of legal rules which are generally considered to be applicable irrespective of the law governing the employment relation, as well as those with respect to which there are divergences of practice and of views. In that connection reference can be made, in particular, to the list, in article 8 of the draft EEC regulation on conflict of laws in employment relations, of legal provisions of the country of the place of work which must be applied in all circumstances; while that list is not at present in any way authoritative, and has been criticised for certain omissions (for instance regarding provisions on equality of treatment),[103] it is claimed in the covering report to correspond to the practice of the countries concerned.[104] It should also be recalled that where international labour Conventions place an obligation on ratifying countries to make certain minimum requirements effective in their territory, the corresponding legal provisions may need to be imperatively applied to all work in that territory.

There would seem to be little doubt regarding the mandatory applicability to all work within the territory of the "forum" of two categories of legal provisions which are protective and which normally need to be implemented collectively in relation to the workforce at any place of work: these categories comprise legal provisions regarding occupational safety and health, and those relating to hours of work, weekly rest and public holidays (*(a)*, *(b)* and *(e)* of the EEC list). The volume and scope of such provisions do, of course, vary from country to country.

It also appears to be generally accepted that the same is true of the mainly prohibitive provisions designed to protect vulnerable groups of workers such as children, young persons, women and the handicapped (*(f)* of the EEC list).

Partly because of the collective nature of labour-management relations, legal provisions on that subject are independent of the law applicable to the individual contract of employment. Nevertheless, it has not been self-evident that all national legislation in the matter need be applied to foreign undertakings operating within the country. The question has been tested in the courts in two countries. In France, a full bench of the Conseil d'Etat held, on 29 June 1973, that compliance with statutory requirements regarding the setting up of a central works council was in France an inherent part of the responsibilities of an employer; only the means of so doing could be adapted to the fact that the employer's principal place of business was abroad.[105] Similarly, in the Federal Republic of Germany, there have been decisions of the Federal Labour Court (of 1 October 1974 and 9 November 1977) affirming that foreign companies are bound by the requirements of the law of the Federal Republic regarding the setting up of a finance committee and consultation of a works council;[106] in the latter case the Court left open the situation of a foreign undertaking employing foreign workers only. No doubt largely because the relevant institutions have not been set up, the subject is not dealt with comprehensively in the legislation that has been expressly made mandatory. The draft EEC regulation would limit mandatory requirements in this field to provisions regarding the protection of workers' representatives.

The greatest divergences of practice and of views relate to categories of legal provisions which bear on matters of a more markedly contractual nature than those covered by the foregoing categories (in particular wages, paid holidays and dismissal).

In much of the legislation referred to earlier in this section, there are provisions concerning the determination of minimum wage rates as well as concerning the protection of wages. In Great Britain, where the parties are left much freedom in this field, mandatory legislation contains provisions regarding certain guarantee payments such as in the event of economic layoff or sick leave.[107] It has been suggested that, where wage rates laid down by collective agreements are made generally applicable, they should be regarded as mandatory at the place of work irrespective of the law applicable to the employment relation. The draft EEC regulation would make provisions on guaranteed minimum wages and salary payments binding.

The EEC draft would also make binding minimum requirements regarding holidays. This may be an area in which ratification of international labour Conventions could play a role. The subject is dealt with in most of the various items of legislation mentioned earlier in this section, except the British Acts. There is some case law which, on the contrary, applies the law of the contractual relation to holiday entitlements;[108] this does not, however, necessarily preclude the compulsory application of local minima. In a 1970 decision a Belgian commercial court applied Belgian law on holiday pay to a contract performed in Belgium but subject to the law of the United States.[109]

All of the various enactments mentioned earlier in this section contain provisions relating to termination of employment. In some other countries there is case law affirming the mandatory character of relevant legislation. Thus in Belgium, decisions of the Court of Cassation of 25 June 1975 [110] and of the Labour Court and Labour Court of Appeals of Brussels, of 10 June 1976 [111] and 20 December 1978 [112] respectively, have asserted that provisions applicable as laws concerning public order and security include those bearing on minimum periods of notice and compensation in lieu of notice. In France, also, any dismissal for economic reasons must comply with French law.[113] On the other hand, courts in the Federal Republic of Germany have held that the Republic's protective legislation relating to dismissals is not mandatorily applicable to work performed in the Federal Republic under a contract governed by foreign law; [114] what is applicable even in such a case is the requirement of consultation of the works council.[115] In Italy there have been a number of decisions affirming that neither periods of notice nor the financially considerable long-service grants payable on termination of employment are measures of public policy of such importance as to be applicable to work carried out in Italy under an employment relation governed by foreign law.[116] In the Netherlands the test for the applicability of a decree of 1945 concerning dismissals is not the law applicable to the employment relation, but whether the Netherlands labour market is affected by the dismissal.[117] The draft EEC regulation would make binding only legal provisions regarding the authorisation of a public authority. This may cover the cases of employees enjoying special protection in relation to dismissal, such as workers' representatives, pregnant women and handicapped workers; in some countries in which general protective provisions in the matter are not regarded as imperative, it appears to be accepted that provisions establishing such special protection override the law of the contract.

Legal provisions made imperatively applicable will be applied, barring anything to the contrary in their express terms, in the entire territory of the country concerned, including, normally, the ships flying its flag.[118] A particular problem arises, however, as regards ships flying a foreign flag in a country's ports and territorial waters. Traditionally, local law was not applied to the internal organisation of such ships. This has been called in question, in particular, as regards employment injuries.[119] Thus in 1973 a Scottish Court applied local law to a claim in respect of the death in Scottish waters of a Norwegian seaman working on a Norwegian-owned vessel under a contract expressly made subject to Norwegian law.[120] In 1970, the Supreme Court of the United States similarly applied United States law (the Jones Act) to an injury suffered in a port in the United States by a

Greek seafarer serving under a contract expressly made subject to Greek law and on board a ship flying the Greek flag.[121] In that case, however, the determining factors were the fact that the owner of the vessel was domiciled in the United States and that the entire income from its operations derived from cargo originating or terminating in that country; the main concern of the Court appears to have been not to permit the evasion of obligations normally lying upon United States citizens and permanent residents by registration abroad. For other cases, the view expressed in an earlier Supreme Court decision,[122] that "to impose upon ships the duty of shifting from one standard of compensation to another as the vessel passes the boundaries of territorial waters would not only be an onerous but also an unduly speculative burden", may well hold good. In a series of decisions in 1963 [123] the Supreme Court also held the National Labor Relations Act to be inapplicable to ships flying a foreign flag, even while in United States waters. On the other hand some account has to be taken of the ILO Merchant Shipping (Minimum Standards) Convention, 1976, which, in article 4, empowers States which have ratified it to take certain steps to ensure the application of its standards on foreign ships entering their ports even if the flag State has not ratified the Convention.[124] It was understood that what would be applied was exclusively the Convention standard, and not the local law as such; [125] nevertheless, use of the power may be tantamount to the imperative application of such elements of the local law as give effect to the Convention standard.

As part of the extension of jurisdiction to offshore operations, particularly on the continental shelf, steps have also been taken in a number of countries to apply to such operations legal provisions in the field of employment the application of which is imperative whether by the terms of such provisions themselves or otherwise. Thus the British Employment Protection (Consolidation) Act, 1978, in particular, is made applicable by the Employment Protection (Offshore Employment) Order, 1976, as amended in 1977 and 1981; a 1977 order also extends the scope of the Health and Safety at Work Act, 1974. A Norwegian royal decree of 24 June 1977 makes applicable to fixed offshore installations the Act of 1977 relating to worker protection and the working environment. Legal provisions regarding safety, minimum age for employment, and hours of work and rest periods are made applicable by the Netherlands regulations in pursuance of the Continental Shelf Mining Act, 1965. In a decision of 21 December 1982 the District Court of Haarlem regarded the fact of employment on the continental shelf off the coast of the Netherlands as one of a number of elements justifying the application of the decree on dismissals to the dismissal of a Chilean worker.[126] In the United States the Occupational Safety and Health Act, 1970, the Fair Labor Standards Act and provisions of the National Labor Relations Act are made applicable either by their own terms or by the Outer Continental Shelf Lands Act.

The continental shelf still represents a case in which the law of the forum is applied to work within the (extended) territorial jurisdiction of the country. There are cases in which an endeavour is made to render the application of that law imperative even for work carried out abroad. Sometimes this endeavour is based on the worker's nationality. Thus the Spanish "Workers' Charter" of 10 March 1980 [127] provides that "Spanish legislation shall apply to the work done by Spanish workers recruited in Spain for service with Spanish undertakings abroad, without prejudice to the principles of public policy applicable at the place of their employment. Such workers shall enjoy at least the financial rights to which they would be entitled if they were employed on Spanish territory". It thus overrides the provisions contained in the New Preliminary Provisions of the Civil Code with regard to both party choice and the proper law of contracts of employment. Similarly, Venezuelan Decree No. 1563 to make regulations under the Labour Act, of 31 December 1973,[128] provides that the provisions of the Act and of international labour Conventions ratified by Venezuela that grant advantages to workers are an integral part of contracts concluded by Venezuelans for service abroad. Sometimes the imperative application of the law of the forum to work abroad is based on the nationality of the undertaking. Thus article 44 of the Yugoslav federal Constitution provides that workers in an organisation of associated labour (i.e. a Yugoslav undertaking) operating abroad shall have the same rights, duties and responsibilities as the workers of the organisation working in Yugoslavia. By reference to that provision the Yugoslav Constitutional Court on 12 July 1977 put in doubt the validity of rules under which workers employed by a Yugoslav engineering undertaking on a hydro-electric project abroad worked 48 hours a week, in accordance with the law of the place of work, whereas in Yugoslavia normal weekly hours would have been 42.[129] A United States federal district court in 1980 held the Civil Rights Act, 1964, to be applicable to a sex discrimination dispute between United States nationals working in Iran and their United States employer, on the ground that the terms of the Act made it inapplicable only to aliens abroad and that, accordingly, a United States employer employing United States nationals had the same obligations abroad as in the United States.[130] It is also on the basis of the nationality of the undertaking that there has been question of the home State of multinational enterprises making certain imperative provisions of its labour law applicable to operations of the enterprise elsewhere.[131] However, there is little evidence that this is being done in practice.

The law of States other than that of the forum

It is one thing for the State of the forum to give effect to its own law, even where it purports to regulate situations outside its territory; it is quite another for it to recognise the imperative nature of particular substantive rules of the law of another State.[132] Again, a distinction has to be made according to whether the legal system in question is that which would be regarded as applicable in the State of the forum in the absence of party choice or not.

Where the legal system in question is, but for party choice, the "proper law", what is involved is the acceptance in the State of the forum of the desirability of applying the imperative provisions of that law, at any rate as a minimum protection, despite the choice of another legal system by the parties. Countries bound by the EEC Convention on the Law Applicable to Contractual Obligations would be obliged to accept this principle by article 6, paragraph 1, to the effect that "in a contract of employment a choice of law made by the parties shall not have the result of depriving the employee of the protection afforded to him by the mandatory rules of the law which would be applicable under paragraph 2 in the absence of choice". The Convention does not spell out which rules are to be regarded as mandatory; the report on the Convention refers, inter alia, to safety and health legislation and to collective agreements which have been made binding. As indicated earlier, the draft of a special regulation contemplates the inclusion therein of a list of legal provisions of the place of work the application of which cannot be exluded; such a list would be binding on the States concerned in their mutual relations only, whereas the rule in the Convention is intended to be general.

The approach of the Austrian federal Act of 1978 on private international law is similar: section 44 (3) provides that, to the extent that mandatory provisions of the law designated by paragraphs (1) and (2) as applicable to the employment relation are involved, even an express choice of law must be disregarded if it was made to the detriment of the employee. In the United States, under the second *Restatement of the Law*, in its volume on conflict of laws, the fundamental policy of the system of law which would apply in the absence of choice prevails if the state concerned has a materially greater interest in the determination of the issue than the state of the chosen law (section 187).

The courts have on occasion referred to the need to respect mandatory provisions of the law of a foreign place of work where it is different from the chosen law, but have not (except perhaps in the United States) [133] found it necessary to apply it in fact. This has been the case, for instance, in Belgium [134] and in France.[135] There may be several reasons for the relative dearth of judicial practice. First, express choice of law by the parties is said not to be very widespread (though it may be becoming so), and the search for implied choice may often lead to the same law as that which would be applicable in the absence of choice. Secondly, it may be that it is mainly in cases in which the chosen law or the law of the forum is more favourable to the claimant that disputes are brought to the courts of a country other than the one the law of which would be applicable in the absence of choice: where the mandatory provisions of the law otherwise applicable are regarded as a protective minimum, they will not, in these circumstances, be applied in practice. Thirdly, in countries which know the distinction, the mandatory provisions are often "public" rather than "private" law, and it is only in very recent years that the possibility of applying foreign public law has not been rejected everywhere as a matter of principle. There remain many aspects of administrative regulation which it is impracticable to apply abroad.

What of the imperative legal provisions of a country other than the forum, where the legal system of that country is neither chosen by the parties nor applicable under the general rules of private international law of the forum? The question can arise above all where the work is performed in that country, but the forum considers the "proper law" to be that of the seat of the undertaking elsewhere, or gives greater importance to connecting factors such as the common nationality of the parties or the place of conclusion of the contract. There are, however, other circumstances which may pose the problem, for instance where, as in the case of the Spanish and Venezuelan provisions cited above, the country of the worker's nationality or domicil seeks to provide a protection not available under the law of the other countries concerned.

The application of the law of such a third State appears to have been first contemplated in the United States. Section 196 of the volume on conflict of laws in the second *Restatement of the Law* provides for the application, in the absence of choice by the parties, of the law of the state where the services are rendered "unless, with respect to the particular issue, some other state has a more significant relationship . . . to the transaction and the parties, in which event the local law of the other state will be applied". Even there (i.e. as between states of a federation, having a great deal of law in common), cases in which the law so applied (for instance that of the domicil of the employee) is not also that of the forum are hard to find.

The EEC Convention on the Law Applicable to Contractual Obligations tentatively enunciates a similar concept. Article 7, paragraph 1, provides that "when applying under this Convention the law of a country, effect may be given to the mandatory rules of the law of another country with which the situation has a close connection, if and in so far as, under the law of the latter country, those rules must be applied whatever the law applicable to the contract. In considering whether to give effect to these mandatory rules, regard shall be had to their nature and purpose and to the consequences of their application or non-application". That the rules in question are not those of the forum is made clear by paragraph 2 of the article, which deals separately with the mandatory law of the forum. Significantly, article 7, paragraph 1, is one of two provisions which a State may on ratification reserve the right not to apply (article 22). The Swiss Bill on private international law, as submitted to Parliament, also envisages the possibility of applying the mandatory provisions of the law of a third State. There is, again, some case law which accepts the principle of the application of such foreign mandatory provisions (particularly a much-cited decision, in 1966, of the Supreme Court of the Netherlands) [136] but does not find it necessary to do so in fact. Probably the most that can be said at present is that there is a readiness in some quarters, but by no means all, to apply the law of a third State should it be shown, in particular cases, that such application would serve the interests of justice.

The most favourable law

As has been seen, the EEC Convention on the Law Applicable to Contractual Obligations conceives the mandatory provisions of the law which would be applicable in the absence of party choice as a protection of which the employee cannot be deprived; by implication, they can be improved upon. This is made crystal clear in the draft of an EEC regulation: article 8, paragraph 3, expressly provides that the law chosen by the parties prevails where it is more favourable to the worker than the mandatory provisions of the place of work (applicable in the absence of choice). The Austrian legislation on private international law, and some of the case law which has referred to the applicability of foreign mandatory provisions, similarly treat such provisions as a minimum standard.

Where the mandatory provisions are those of the forum, whether they are treated as a minimum or as a rule which cannot be altered, for good as well as for bad, would seem to depend on their terms and their interpretation. Writers in a number of countries affirm that the mandatory provisions of their own countries can generally be improved upon either by the law chosen by the parties or by the (foreign) law applicable in the absence of party choice.[137] The relative absence of case law can perhaps be explained on the ground that – barring the few examples of legislation expressly made applicable irrespective of the law of the contract – the positive public policy of the State of the forum will mainly be invoked where it improves on the law chosen or otherwise applicable.

It would nevertheless be an over-simplification to consider that it is possible in all cases to give the worker the benefit of the law most favourable to him.

First of all, while in certain respects (e.g. an entitlement to two, three, or four weeks of paid holidays) it is easy to "improve" on the mandatory rule, the same is not true where different systems of law deal with the same issue in a different manner. For instance, such a situation raises the question of the extent to which a worker may cumulate benefits: for example, may he benefit from the long period of notice of termination of one system of law together with the more substantial severance pay of another? That question can be studied in wider terms by reference to the extent to which the advantages and disadvantages of a particular legal system are interrelated.

Secondly, even where the two systems of law at issue are comparable, the mandatory provisions can be improved upon only in so far as such an improvement is within the power of the parties. For instance, where the longer holidays or maternity leave, or the better severance indemnities, of the chosen law are paid for out of public funds the worker will be entitled to them only if his situation falls within the rules of eligibility of these funds. This is a specific illustration of the fact, referred to earlier, that in choosing a system of law the limitations on the scope of some of its elements may have to be accepted.

Thirdly, as has been seen, a large part of the legal provisions generally accepted as mandatory call for collective application. It is difficult to envisage improvement, by party choice or otherwise, of the legal provisions mandatorily applicable at the place of work with regard to workers' representation, for instance. In that connection it might be noted that the improvement on local rules regarding hours of work envisaged in the decision of the Yugoslav Constitutional Court referred to above would be a collective one, i.e. one applicable to all workers employed by the Yugoslav undertaking abroad.

There is also the problem of equality of treatment of workers doing comparable jobs. It is widely considered that international agreements providing for equality of treatment of migrant workers are designed to establish a minimum; this is indeed often clear from their terminology.[138] The same is not true of much national legislation designed to prevent discrimination; equality of treatment is there intended to be a matter of precise comparability. Irrespective of whether such legislation is mandatory in relation to contracts of employment governed by foreign law (as some is, for instance, in Great Britain), advantages given to one worker under foreign law may give other workers a claim to be treated alike. The only reason why the problem of equality of treatment is perhaps not of overriding importance in the present context is that, by and large, workers whose employment relations are subject to foreign law are not in jobs comparable to those of nationals of the country of assignment.

Finally, however important the aim of giving workers favourable treatment may be as a matter of public policy, there are other community concerns which may, on occasion, conflict with that aim. For instance, there may be mandatory provisions not only on guaranteed minimum wages, but also on the limitation of wage increases. Moreover, in certain fields of labour law the respective rights and obligations of employers and workers are carefully balanced (for instance in the law regarding the contractual prohibition of competition or disclosure of trade secrets, which is regarded by some as being a matter of public policy). It would seem to be difficult in such cases to allow the law to be improved upon for the benefit of one of the parties only.

D. REFUSAL TO APPLY FOREIGN LAW

It is universally accepted that the State of the "forum" may refuse to apply particular elements of foreign law, whether that law be chosen by the parties or otherwise applicable, if to do so would run counter to its own "public policy". This principle is a reflection of the fact that the rules of private international law, which decide when and to what extent foreign law shall be applied, are a branch of national law.

Most legislation on private international law contains an express provision reserving this power. The terms in which it does so vary somewhat. Under the most common language, the "public policy and good morals" of the country are protected. There are, however, cases in which the notion of "public policy" or certain aspects of it are made more explicit. For instance, Brazil and Guatemala specify, inter alia, that foreign law shall not be applied if such application would run counter to national sovereignty. Reference to political or social institutions is made in the additional protocol to the 1940 Montevideo Treaties on private international law and in the legislation of Albania, Czechoslovakia and the German Democratic Republic. The legislation of the German Democratic Republic also attaches importance in this connection to conflict with its legal order, and so does the legislation of Austria and Poland. Under the legislation of Argentina and Nicaragua, foreign law will not be applied if it runs counter to public law or the spirit of the Civil Code; similarly, the legislation of the Federal Republic of Germany provides that no foreign law shall be applied if its application offends against the intent of a law of the Federal Republic.

Generally, what is at issue is not the nature and content of the foreign law as such but the consequences of its application by the State of the forum. The report on the EEC Convention on the Law Applicable to Contractual Obligations draws attention to the wording of article 16, under which application of a rule of the law of any country specified by the Convention may be refused only if such application conflicts with the public policy of the State of the forum. The language of some national legislation on private international law similarly stresses that what must be considered is the effect of application of the foreign rule: the Austrian Act of 1978 provides that foreign law shall not be applied if the result would be irreconcilable with the basic tenets of the Austrian legal order; the Czechoslovak law of 1963 specifies that foreign law shall be excluded to the extent that its application would be contrary to the principles of the social and political system of the country; the 1975 law of the German Democratic Republic is analogous in tenor; the Polish statute of 1966 provides that foreign law shall not be applied "if its application would produce effects" contrary to the fundamental principles of the national legal order; under the Portuguese legislative decree of 1966 provisions of foreign law shall not be applied if their application would involve violation of the fundamental principles of the international public policy of Portugal; the Spanish decree of 1964 and the Swiss Bill as submitted to Parliament also look to the result of application. This is also the approach of some case law. For instance, in its decision of 10 April 1975 [139] the Federal Labour Court of the Federal Republic of Germany stated that "only where the application of the foreign law would lead to obviously intolerable results" should recourse be had to the public policy proviso of the introduction to the Civil Code. Normally this means that only the effects within the territory of the country of the forum of the application of the foreign law will be taken into account. It may nevertheless be that there are legal provisions which are so repugnant not only to national public policy but to internationally accepted principles of justice that they should not be applied irrespective of whether application directly involves the territory of the forum. In the labour field, provisions involving slavery, forced labour or other forms of bondage come to mind. Significantly, the Código Bustamante declares the prohibition of contracts for life or for more than a specified period to be a matter of international public policy (article 197).

It would also appear that there can be question of refusing to apply foreign law only where fundamental principles are at issue. As can be seen from the citations in the preceding paragraph, this is made clear by the express terms of the legislation on private international law of Austria, Czechoslovakia, the German Democratic Republic, Poland and Portugal; the same is also true of the legislation of Uruguay and the USSR. The EEC Convention on the Law Applicable to Contractual Obligations would permit refusal to apply foreign law only where such application would be "manifestly incompatible" with the public policy of the State of the forum; analogous language was used in the French draft legislation of 1969. Some case law has also affirmed that "public policy" is the complex of fundamental ethical and legal principles on which the national community is based.[140]

The limitations on recourse to the public policy proviso mean that cases in which the application of foreign law is refused by reference to it are not frequent. In their decisions referred to in the foregoing paragraphs, the courts of the Federal Republic of Germany and of Italy took the view that the provisions regarding termination of employment of the law governing the employment relation, different though they were from the national law of the State of the forum, could not be considered to be contrary to public policy. An Italian court has further held that it is not against public policy to limit the right to strike on ships flying the Liberian flag.[141] There would seem to be three main fields in which some courts have shown an inclination not to apply the foreign law governing the employment relation. The first consists of discriminatory provisions. In a decision dating from 1937, the Swiss Federal Tribunal refused to recognise the validity of a dismissal based on German racial legislation, while the Austrian Supreme Court in 1951 and 1955 took a similar attitude to dismissals in Czechoslovakia based on the national extraction of the employee.[142] A second is that of legal provisions which, in the eyes of the judges of the forum, permit excessive limitations on the freedom of employees to compete with a former employer or to disclose information acquired in employment. There is recent case law on this in the United States;[143] decisions elsewhere are old and open to criticism.[144] Thirdly, there are provisions governing the limitation of the rights of employees to bring civil claims for employment injuries. For instance, in the United States the second *Restatement of the Law* provides (in section 184 of the volume on conflict of laws) for the universal recognition of immunity from such claims given to defendants who are required to take out insurance cover (i.e. normally the employer), but leaves open to question whether the immunity given in some states to fellow-employees will be recognised elsewhere. Reference was made in section C above to a Scottish case in which a limitation of liability under Norwegian law was not taken into account, as contrary to Scottish law.

Where a particular provision of foreign law is not applied, the question arises: what should be put in its place? Some legislation on private international law specifies that the law of the forum shall then be applied. This is the case, for instance, in the German Democratic Republic, Hungary and Kuwait. The express provisions of Austrian and Portuguese legislation are more flexible: the corresponding rule of Austrian law is applied "if necessary", while Portuguese law is applied "subsidiarily", the main part of the relevant provision requiring the application of the most suitable rules of the law governing the relation at issue. Such a flexible approach also seems to be followed in some countries which do not have legislation on this point. An example of what this means in practice is provided by a decision of the Argentine National Labour Appeals Court of 21 March 1975.[145] A fatal employment injury on board a ship was found to be governed by the Norwegian law of the flag. The amount of benefit due in respect of such an injury under that law was different for Norwegian citizens and for aliens. The Court ignored the special provision for aliens, on the ground that it was discriminatory and hence contrary to public policy, and applied Norwegian law as it would have applied to a Norwegian citizen.

A completely different type of refusal to apply foreign law has been mentioned earlier (in connection both with the elements of foreign law covered by the choice of the parties, and with the application of the mandatory law of a country other than that of the forum), namely refusals to apply certain types of foreign "public" law. In this comparative survey, reference to the concept of "public" as opposed to "private" law is as far as possible being avoided, for several reasons: in some countries (in particular the Common Law countries and the socialist countries) no formal distinction is made; even countries which make the distinction accept that the private law consequences of public law requirements can be given effect abroad; in any case, the notion that it is impossible to give effect to foreign public law is no longer generally adhered to. Yet two problems remain; one is practical and the other is a matter of policy. The practical problem, already referred to, is that where foreign law requires the intervention of a public authority (for instance to authorise the termination of the employment of particular categories of protected persons) it is not possible to apply it, as such, abroad (although account can be taken of the failure to obtain the authorisation, as appropriate). The policy problem may be summarised as follows: the application of foreign law is the result of the generally accepted desirability of international co-operation in promoting the stability of private legal relationships; co-operation does not normally extend to the enforcement of foreign law which serves the specific interests of the foreign State; thus foreign penal and revenue laws will generally not be applied, although they may be taken into account in determining, for instance, whether it was impossible to perform an obligation prohibited by them; what is the relevance, in the labour field, of the fact that the primary purpose of some legal provision is to protect a national labour market or a national economy? To take a specific example: where an undertaking with branches in a number of countries is unable to pay, in one of them, the full contractually agreed wage because of mandatory local anti-inflation legislation, will compliance with this legislation constitute a defence to a claim for the remainder at its principal place of business, and is there any difference in the reply to that question according to whether the law applicable to the employment relation is that of the country in which the anti-inflation legislation was adopted or whether that legislation overrode a foreign applicable law? There are no ready answers to this question at present, perhaps because the difficulties are being avoided in practice, but this in no way precludes their potential importance.

E. JURISDICTION

It will be apparent from the foregoing that the answer to a problem regarding an international employment relation may differ according to the "forum" in which the problem comes before a court. In particular, different criteria may be used to determine the applicable law, and the substantive provisions of national law treated as imperative may differ. There may even be a different starting-point: the first step is to decide the nature of the problem (so-called primary classification), and the answer is not always self-evident: for instance, a contractual limitation on the liability of the employer may be seen either as a contractual problem or as one in civil liability. In all these circumstances, it is of some importance to know which courts and administrative authorities have jurisdiction to deal with the matter.

There are considerable divergences amongst States on the approaches to this question. Several criteria are used, sometimes in combination. Many of them lead to what is regarded elsewhere as an excessively wide claim to jurisdiction.

Some countries place key emphasis on nationality as a factor establishing jurisdiction. This is so, for instance, in France [146] and a number of French-speaking African countries. [147] It means that nationals may sue and be sued in their own country, in disputes with non-resident foreigners, even where the subject of the dispute has no other relation with it. The option that this gives to a worker to sue in his home country with respect to work carried out abroad is also found, for instance, in Brazil [148] and in the German Democratic Republic.[149] It is paralleled, for instance in Belgium, Italy and the Netherlands, by provisions enabling a person to sue at the place of his domicil; [150] the draft Swiss law on private international law as submitted to Parliament gives that faculty specifically to workers claiming under a contract of employment. There has, moreover, been case law in some countries which do not use nationality as a main criterion, under which the fact that the employee is a national, or that both parties are, is used to establish the jurisdiction of a court in labour matters.[151]

A second group of countries uses the habitual residence of the defendant as the main basis for jurisdiction. This is so in Austria,[152] the Federal Republic of Germany,[153] Japan,[154] the Netherlands,[155] Norway [156] and Switzerland,[157] as well as in the majority of the socialist countries of Eastern Europe.[158] Some of the countries concerned also assume jurisdiction if the defendant has assets in the country, wherever he may be domiciled and irrespective of whether the subject of the dispute has any relation to these assets.

A third main tendency is that of the Anglo-Saxon countries and of those – such as some English-speaking African countries – which apply certain of their principles of private international law. Court jurisdiction is there treated as a procedural matter, based on the service on the defendant of papers initiating the action. This means that action is possible in relation to persons only temporarily in the country, or to undertakings having an agent there, irrespective of the relationship between the work of the agent and the subject of the dispute. The latter aspect has been particularly developed in United States practice under so-called "long arm" laws. At the same time, the limitations of this method are avoided by procedural rules permitting service of papers abroad in cases in which the dispute has specified links with the country.

Whatever may be the main basis for the exercise of jurisdiction, nearly everywhere there are also grounds related to the substance of the issue in dispute. In particular, the place either of conclusion or of performance of a contract is widely regarded as a basis for jurisdiction over disputes relating to that contract. In some countries it is expressly specified that there is jurisdiction over disputes regarding an employment relation at the place where the work is carried out.[159] In any case there is little doubt that the administrative authorities (especially the inspection services) of the place of work have competence to deal with questions regarding the application at least of mandatory legislation regarding such matters as safety and health and basic conditions of work.

The wide range of grounds for the exercise of jurisdiction means not only that several options may be open to the aggrieved party in a dispute, but also that the authorities of several countries may be seized simultaneously. There are three main means of meeting the problem: desistment of the authorities of one country in favour of those of another; international agreements; and choice by the parties of an exclusive forum.

There are some grounds on which it may be open to courts to decide that they will not proceed with the consideration of a particular dispute: because the matter is already before the courts of another country *(lis alibi pendens)* or because it is more appropriate for it to be considered elsewhere *(forum non conveniens)*. A court which was the first to be seized may even prohibit the introduction of proceedings elsewhere. However, even where courts have these powers – and they do not have them universally – they are reluctant to exercise them. For instance, in a number of countries courts will desist from proceeding with a case only if it is certain that the decision of the foreign court seized of the matter will be recognised in their own country. Also, it appears to be felt that the possibility open to a plaintiff to get a greater advantage should not be lightly interfered with; for instance, in a decision of 1980, a majority of the English Court of Appeal saw no objection to the seeking of a remedy in the United States by a plaintiff severely injured in an occupational accident, even though interim damages had already been paid in England, on the ground that it would be less than humane to deny him the opportunity to pursue his claim to compensation wherever it would evoke the most generous response.[160] Nevertheless, courts do sometimes refuse to consider a case. For instance, again in England, the House of Lords decided in 1978, in a number of consolidated claims by Scottish workers regarding injuries suffered at their place of work in Scotland, that Scotland was the proper forum even though English courts had jurisdiction by virtue of the fact that the employing companies were registered in England.[161] It may be that such a conclusion is more readily arrived at as between the different legal systems of a single sovereign State.

There are international treaties, both multilateral and bilateral, which seek to define and limit the grounds of judicial competence. Thus the 1968 Brussels (European Economic Community) Convention on jurisdiction and the enforcement of judgements in civil and commercial matters [162] makes the domicil of the defendant [163] the main ground for the exercise of jurisdiction; there are, in addition, some special grounds which include, for contracts, the place where the obligation was or should have been performed. Other grounds recognised in the States concerned are expressly excluded. The Convention applies to labour matters, but has no special provisions on the subject.[164] Analogous grounds for jurisdiction, inter alia in labour matters, are provided for in the 1940 Montevideo Convention on International Civil Law. Of the many bilateral treaties defining judicial competence, a good number appear not to cover labour matters.[165] The relationship of the various treaties to national law can give rise to difficult questions. As recently as 1977, a full bench of the French Court of Cassation was needed to decide that a provision of a Franco-Swiss treaty of 1869, under which Swiss courts were competent in a dispute between a French commercial representative and his Swiss employer, was superior to internal law and that, accordingly, the public policy nature of the French legislation relating to such representatives could not be relied upon to establish French jurisdiction.[166] The Italian Court of Cassation, in a decision of 11 October 1979 overruling lower courts, held that the Brussels Convention prevailed over a later provision of the Civil Code because the legislature had not expressly indicated the contrary.[167] At the same time, some Italian writers are still posing the question of the compatibility of certain aspects of the Brussels Convention with the Italian Constitution.[168]

The greatest certainty for the parties can be attained by an agreement between them on one exclusive forum. The Brussels Convention of 1968 provides that on condition that one party is domiciled in the European Economic Community a written agreement shall vest sole competence in the forum chosen. It is, however, very controversial whether individuals should have the power, not so much to give competence to a particular forum (prorogation) as to exclude the jurisdiction of an otherwise competent forum (derogation). The question arises first in general terms: in particular, is it possible for the jurisdiction of the established authorities of a State to be excluded by the decision of a private individual? In a number of countries this is not normally possible; for instance, in many socialist countries of Eastern Europe derogation is possible only for economic organisations in connection with international trade. In others, some compromise between extreme positions has been found: this may take the form of permitting individual decision in limited circumstances or fields, or of allowing courts to weigh the reasonableness of the choice made by the parties. Then there is the second question of the appropriateness of allowing a choice by the parties to a contract of employment. The arguments used for and against such choice parallel those for and against party choice of applicable law.[169] The arguments against are often reinforced by provisions in Labour Codes prohibiting internal derogation from the statutory competence of particular courts.[170]

Recent case law in labour matters tends to permit the choice of forum by the parties, but it does so with circumspection and reservations. In a few cases the decisions are the result of the applicability of the Brussels Convention: by a decision of 13 November 1979, the Court of Justice of the European Communities confirmed that under the terms of the Convention choice-of-forum clauses in international contracts of employment are valid;[171] the derogation from national jurisdiction involved was accepted, for instance, by the Italian Court of Cassation in a decision of 11 October 1979.[172] Also, a decision of the Labour Court of Appeal of Brussels, of 4 July 1973, holding valid a clause giving French courts jurisdiction over an employment relation between French nationals for work performed in Belgium, was based in large part on a bilateral treaty.[173] However, other decisions are more general. In France there have been a series of decisions [174] accepting choice-of-forum clauses, but only as regards contracts concluded by French employees with foreign companies for work abroad. In the Federal Republic of Germany the Federal Labour Court has affirmed that choice-of-forum clauses are valid, but only in so far as an individual need for protection does not require the contrary; [175] it has quoted approvingly, though without immediate relevance to the cases before it, the view of certain writers that the jurisdiction of the courts of the Federal Republic cannot be excluded if the work is carried out in that country and if the employee is not at least of a middle-management grade. The only example of actual disregard of a choice-of-forum clause by the Federal Labour Court may be found in a decision of 26 June 1978; [176] in a claim by a national of the Federal Republic who was resident in Lebanon against his Lebanese employer the exclusion of the jurisdiction of the courts of the Federal Republic by such a choice was held to be void, on the ground that the courts of the chosen forum (Beirut) were not in a position to act because of a state of war and that hence there would be no remedy under the contract. In Sweden, the Labour Court in 1976 held that generally an agreement to give competence to a foreign court was valid even in labour matters, but that there were circumstances in the case before it justifying a departure from the general rule; the circumstances relied on were that the work was performed in Sweden, that the act complained of (dismissal) affected the Swedish labour market, and that the substantive law applicable was the mandatory Employment Protection Act.[177]

There is one overriding consideration in choosing a forum, either by agreement or as a claimant, namely that it will be possible to give effect to the decision. This will normally be the case either if satisfaction can be obtained at the place at which the decision is given or if the decision will be recognised in another country for the purpose of enforcement. There are many limitations on the recognition of foreign judgements. In some countries recognition is given only to the extent provided for by international agreements. In others, it depends on whether the court was competent to deal with the matter under the criteria applied in the State asked for recognition. In any case, if recognition has to be obtained it will be necessary to take action twice, with increased costs and protracted proceedings. In some situations, such as those of "double migration", the employer has no continuing contacts either with the country of the place of work or with that in which the worker was recruited; in such cases an application for recognition of the judgement of a foreign court may unfortunately be the only means of achieving results.

Notes

[1] Joost Blom: "Choice of law methods in the private international law of contract", in *Can. Yearb. Int. Law*, 1978, pp. 230-275; 1979, pp. 206-246; 1980, pp. 161-200.

[2] For the most comprehensive recent review of the subject see A. Curti Gialdino: "La volonté des parties en droit international privé", in *Cours Acad. droit int.*, 1972, III, pp. 751-921.

[3] Hudson: *International legislation*, Vol. 8: *1938-1941* (Washington, DC, 1949), pp. 529-532.

[4] For instance, article 35 of the 1970 Argentine draft code on private international law and article 29 of the Venezuelan draft of 1965. See also E. L. Fermé, in Chapter VII of Vasquez Vialard (ed.): *Tratado de derecho del trabajo*, Vol. II (Buenos Aires, 1982), affirming that under existing Argentine law the parties may decide the law applicable to international contracts.

[5] An express choice is required by article 10 (5) of the new preliminary provisions of the Spanish Civil Code and by Hungarian Legislative Decree No. 13 of 1979.

[6] The Czechoslovak Act of 1963 on international civil law requires that "in view of the circumstances, there shall be no doubt as to [the parties'] manifested will" (section 9).

[7] The Austrian Private International Law Act of 1976 provides that "if the circumstances reveal that the parties have assumed a particular legal order as determinative" this shall be equivalent to an implied selection (section 35 (1)).

[8] Whereas in a few countries, such as the Federal Republic of Germany, the choice of a jurisdiction is regarded as virtually tantamount to a choice of law, others regard it merely as one factor among many to be taken into account.

[9] See for instance the note by H. Batiffol in *Rev. crit.*, 1980, pp. 576 ff., on a decision of the French Court of Cassation of 25 March 1980.

[10] For a summary of relevant case law see A. Curti Gialdino, loc. cit. (note 2 above), at pp. 874-875. On the issue of principle see Tomaszewski: "La désignation postérieure à la conclusion du contrat de la loi qui le régit", in *Rev. crit.*, 1972, pp. 567 ff.

[11] O. Kahn-Freund: "General problems of private international law", in *Cours Acad. droit int.*, 1974, III, Ch. V.

[12] See also Sudanese case law, analysed in "Chronique de jurisprudence africaine", "Afrique noire anglophone", in *Clunet*, 1975, pp. 120 ff.

[13] For instance, in British and Nigerian case law.

[14] See the report on the convention by M. Giuliano and P. Lagarde, in *Official Journal of the European Communities*, C. 282/1980.

[15] In 1975 the Institute of International Law stated that the so-called principle of the inapplicability *a priori* of foreign public law was based on no cogent theoretical or practical reason, and considered that the fact that a provision of foreign law designated by the rule of conflict of laws was deemed to fall within the sphere of public law should not prevent the application of that provision. The Swiss Bill on private international law, as submitted to Parliament, expressly affirms this in article 13 (3).

[16] This problem was relevant to some French decisions in the field of employment: Court of Cassation, 31 May 1972 (*Rev. crit.*, 1973, p. 683); and Court of Appeal of Rennes, 8 Dec. 1977 (*Clunet*, 1978, p. 885).

[17] Some legislation on private international law (e.g. that of Albania, Egypt, Italy and Greece) does not permit *renvoi* at all. But in a number of countries in which it is normally accepted, *renvoi* is not admissible where there is a contractual choice of law (e.g. Austria, Czechoslovakia and Portugal; see also the 1967 French draft legislation).

[18] *Sayers* v. *International Drilling Co., N.V.*, [1971] 1 W.L.R. 1176. For a criticism of the decision on the particular issue discussed here, see Lagarde: "'Dépeçage' dans le droit international privé des contrats", in *Riv. dir. int. priv. proc.*, 1975, pp. 649 ff.

[19] See for instance M. L. Deveali: "La relación de trabajo en el derecho internacional privado", in *D° del trabajo*, 1952, p. 65; and M. Simon-Depitre: "Droit du travail et conflits de lois", in *Rev. crit.*, 1958, pp. 285 ff.

[20] For recent work having a bearing on employment relations see W. Fikentscher: "Arbeitsstatut, Prorogation und die zugehörigen Grenzen der Parteiautonomie", in *Recht der Arbeit* (Munich), 1969, pp. 204-208; O. Kahn-Freund and W. Zöllner in *Etudes suisses de droit européen*, Vol. 14 (Geneva, 1973), pp. 201, 213; F. Vischer: "The antagonism between legal security and the search for justice in the field of contracts", in *Cours Acad. droit int.*, 1974, II, pp. 1-65; B. von Hoffman: "Über den Schutz des Schwächeren bei internationalen Schuldverträgen", in *RabelsZ.*, 1974, pp. 396 ff.; O. Lando: "Les obligations contractuelles", in *European private international law of obligations* (Tübingen, 1975); J. Kropholler: "Das kollisionsrechtliche System des Schutzes der schwächeren Vertragspartei", in *RabelsZ.*, 1978, pp. 634-661. It may be that some legislation specifically enacted for the protection of consumers could be relied on in employment relations also; for instance, it is suggested in B. A. Hepple and P. O'Higgins (eds.): *Encyclopedia of labour relations law* (London, Sweet and Maxwell), at 2-1767, that an employee may be able to invoke the provisions of the Unfair Contract Terms Act, 1977, as regards liability in contract (the provisions regarding liability for negligence apply in any case).

[21] This was emphasised in the introductory paper (by I. Szaszy) for the consideration of the subject of conflicts of laws in labour matters by the Institute of International Law, and by some participants (e.g. C. W. Jenks).

[22] See in particular G. Schnorr: *Arbeits- und sozialrechtliche Fragen der europäischen Integration* (Berlin (West), 1974); H. Kronke: "Europäische Vereinheitlichung des Arbeitskollisionsrechts als Wirtschafts- und Sozialpolitik", in *RabelsZ.*, 1981, pp. 301-319.

[23] See in particular S. Simitis: "Internationales Arbeitsrecht: Standort und Perspektiven", in *Festschrift für Gerhard Kegel* (Frankfurt am Main, 1977).

[24] See for instance F. Gamillscheg: "Intereuropäisches Arbeitsrecht", in *RabelsZ.*, 1973, pp. 284-316; G. Beitzke: "EWG-Kollisionsnormen zum Arbeitsverhältnis", in *Gedächtnisschrift für Rolf Dietz* (Munich, 1973).

[25] See for instance B. A. Hepple: "Conflict of laws in employment relationships within the E.E.C.", in K. Lipstein (ed.): *Harmonisation of private international law by the E.E.C.* (London, 1978); G. and A. Lyon-Caen: *Droit social international et européen* (Paris, 5th ed., 1980), reflecting French case law; H. Valladão: *Direito internacional privado*, Vol. III (Rio de Janeiro, 1978), Ch. LXVI, reflecting Brazilian case law; F. Pocar: "La legge applicabile ai rapporti di lavoro secondo il diritto italiano", in *Riv. dir. int. priv. proc.*, 1972, pp. 726-754; W. Däubler: "Grundprobleme des internationalen Arbeitsrechts", in *A.W.D.*, 1972, pp. 8 ff. On the narrower question of the possibility of improving on mandatory legal provisions by party choice see section C of the present chapter.

[26] *Etudes suisses de droit international*, Vol. 12 (Zurich, 1978), at p. 223.

[27] See Beitzke, op. cit. in note 24, and Simitis, op. cit. in note 23.

[28] See F. K. Juenger: "The Conflicts Statute of the German Democratic Republic", in *Amer. J. Compar. Law*, 1977, at p. 350, and K. Buure-Hägglund: "Codification of private international law rules on employment contracts", in *Scand. Studies in Law*, 1980.

[29] *Rev. crit.*, 1981, p. 171, n. 9.

[30] Such choice would be permitted in the event of a transfer from one establishment to another if the employer remains the same; in case of work which is not localised in one place; and in the case of managerial or highly specialised employees.

[31] In the event of transfer from one establishment to another, the choice lies between the law applying to the one or the other. In case of work which is not localised in one place, the choice lies between the law of one of the places of work, that of the permanent residence of the worker, and that of the domicil of the employer or the principal place of business of the undertaking.

[32] See, for instance, a 1977 decision of a New York city court (93 Misc. 2d 818) in which Illinois law, although provided for in the contract, was not applied on this ground to a contract of employment concluded, performed and terminated in New York, the employer being a Delaware corporation.

[33] *Riv. dir. int. priv. proc.*, 1977, p. 890.

[34] See for instance G. and A. Lyon-Caen: *Droit social international et européen* (Paris, 5th ed., 1980); C. Reithmann: *Internationales Vertragsrecht* (Cologne, 3rd ed., 1980); R. Birk: "Internationales Tarifsvertragsrecht", in *Festschrift für Günther Beitzke* (Berlin (West), 1979).

II Notes

[35] See for example R. Birk: "Auslandsbeziehungen und Betriebsverfassungsgesetz", in *Festschrift für Ludwig Schnorr von Carolsfeld* (Cologne, 1972); W. Däubler: "Mitbestimmung und Betriebsverfassung im internationalen Privatrecht", in *RabelsZ.*, 1975, pp. 444 ff.

[36] *Official Journal of the European Communities*, C. 282/1980.

[37] See V. Vannes: "Droit applicable au contrat de travail en présence d'éléments d'extranéité", in *J. Trib. Travail*, 1981, at p. 239.

[38] See H. Valladão: *Direito internacional privado*, Vol. III (Rio de Janeiro, 1978), Ch. LXVI, at p. 100; H. Schwarz: "Problematik internationaler Arbeitsverträge für deutsche Arbeitnehmer in Brasilien", in *R.I.W./A.W.D.*, 1976, p. 50.

[39] In particular, decisions of the Court of Cassation of 31 May 1972 (*Rev. crit.*, 1973, p. 683) and of 3 March 1978 (*Rev. crit.*, 1978, p. 701).

[40] See Buure-Hägglund, op. cit. in note 28.

[41] In the Federal Republic of Germany, unlike England, many writers favour limitations. But the country's case law remains resolutely in favour of party choice: see for instance decisions of the Federal Labour Court of 10 April 1975 (*Int. Labour Law Rep.*, Vol. 2, F.R. Ger. 7), and of 4 May 1977 (*A.P.*, Case No. 30 on section 1 of the Collective Agreements Act (TVG)). So do some authors, such as F. Gamillscheg.

[42] See the cases cited in Ch. I, note 9. However, in a somewhat bizarre decision of 6 September 1980 (*Clunet*, 1983, p. 190), the Court of Cassation appeared to take the view that if in respect of work in Italy the applicable law was less favourable to the worker than Italian law, the latter should apply.

[43] The countries in question are Algeria, Argentina (for contracts concluded outside Argentina and not to be performed there), Brazil, Costa Rica, Egypt, Italy, Gabon, Japan, Morocco, Peru, the Republic of Korea and Thailand. In most of them the place of conclusion is not the primary connecting factor.

[44] See the sources cited in Ch. I, note 12, and see a decision of the Supreme Labour Court of 9 January 1951, summarised by Deveali in *Dº del trabajo*, 1952, p. 65.

[45] See for instance I. Szaszy's introductory paper on the conflict of laws in labour matters in *Ann. Inst. droit int.*, 1971.

[46] The relevant decisions include those of the Court of Appeal of Rome of 29 July 1955 (Egyptian law applied to work abroad); the Tribunal of Milan of 13 July 1961 and 24 November 1966 (Italian law applied to work abroad), of 26 September 1968 (French law applied to work in Italy) and of 29 May 1972 (English law applied to work in Italy); and the court of first instance of La Spezia, of 4 February 1977 (Italian law applied to work in Italy).

[47] See Vannes, op. cit. in note 37, at p. 238. In a number of cases (see for instance *J. Trib. Travail*, 1981, pp. 71-72) the place of conclusion was also that from which instructions were given to the employee abroad.

[48] Decision of 28 May 1982. *Financial Times* (London), 15 June 1982, "Commercial Law Report".

[49] Costa Rica (common nationality), Egypt and Kuwait (common domicil), Italy (common nationality), Morocco (common domicil and common nationality), Portugal (common residence), Thailand (common nationality).

[50] See Vannes, op. cit. in note 37.

[51] The common nationality of the parties was a factor, amongst others, in the decision of the Court of Cassation of 31 May 1972 (*Rev. crit.*, 1973, p. 683).

[52] Decision of 10 April 1975, cited in note 41. It should be noted that the case concerned an airline pilot. For an earlier decision of a regional labour court see *IPRspr.*, 1968-1969, No. 53.

[53] See for instance a decision of the Tribunal of Milan of 26 September 1968 (*Riv. dir. int.*, 1970, pp. 334 ff.): French law was applied to work in Italy on the ground both of the common nationality of the parties and the conclusion of the contract in France. Arguably this case was one of long-term transfer; as will be seen below, the considerations applicable in such a case are not very different.

[54] *Sayers* v. *International Drilling Co., N.V.*, [1971] 1 W.L.R. 1176.

[55] See W. Goldschmidt: "Derecho internacional privado del trabajo", in Deveali (ed.): *Tratado de derecho del trabajo*, Vol. IV (Buenos Aires, 1966), Book X. It can, however, also refer to the registered office of the employing undertaking in particular situations.

[56] The concept of "habitual" performance of work has been criticised. See for instance L. Collins: "Contractual obligations: The EEC preliminary draft convention on private international law", *Int. Compar. Law Q.*, 1976, pp. 35 ff., who suggests that a better test would be the place where the parties contemplate that the employment shall take place.

[57] Other countries stressing the place of performance in their legislation regarding contracts are Guatemala and Uruguay.

[58] *Neth. Int. Law Rev.*, 1974, p. 313. See also a decision of the District Court of Roermond of 15 April 1976 (ibid., 1976, p. 357).

[59] See Vannes, op. cit. in note 37.

[60] The relevant French case law, and in particular the decisions of the Court of Cassation of 31 May 1972 and 31 March 1978, is involved with questions of "implied" party choice and the extent to which it can override the law of the place where the work is carried out.

[61] See Reithmann, op. cit. in note 34, and U. Drobnig: *American-German private international law* (New York, 1972).

[62] *Ann. Inst. droit int.*, 1971.

[63] *Riv. dir. int. priv. proc.*, 1975, p. 737.

[64] See for instance M. Simon-Depitre: "La loi du 3 janvier 1972 sur le travail temporaire et le droit international privé", in *Rev. crit.*, 1973, pp. 277 ff., and A. Lyon-Caen: "La mise à disposition internationale de salariés", in *Droit social*, 1981, pp. 747 ff. The Court of Justice of the European Communities, in a decision of 17 December 1970 (*Dalloz-Sirey*, 1971, "Jurisprudence", pp. 255-257) justified this course on the ground that the temporary work agency was the centre of all legal relations in the case.

[65] In a decision of the Paris Court of Appeal of 4 July 1975 (*Rev. crit.*, 1976, p. 485), French law on holidays with pay was applied to recruitment for a short mission to Yugoslavia.

[66] The European Convention on Social Security, EEC Regulation 1408/71 and the Andean Social Security Instrument provide for 12 months, which may be extended with the agreement of the State where the work is performed; the Convention of the African and Mauritian Common Organisation provides for six months, which may similarly be extended. The Great Lakes Countries Convention provides for 12 months, which may apparently not be extended.

[67] One of the circumstances in respect of which the draft EEC regulation envisages party choice, with a view to allowing the original law to apply, is in the event of transfer between establishments of the same undertaking in different countries.

[68] See for instance A. Lyon-Caen: "La mise à disposition internationale de salariés", in *Droit social*, 1981, pp. 747 ff. This statement does not apply as regards countries such as Italy which do not use the place of performance as a connecting factor. Moreover, the terms of section 44 (1) of the Austrian Act of 1978 appear to make the law of the initial place of performance applicable in case of even long-term transfer, and section 52 (2) of the Hungarian legislative decree of 1979 makes Hungarian law applicable to service abroad for a Hungarian employer, irrespective of the duration of such service.

[69] See for instance a decision of a British industrial tribunal of 4 July 1978, cited in F. Gamillscheg: "Neue Entwicklungen im englischen und europäischen internationalen Arbeitsrecht", in *R.I.W./A.W.D.*, 1979. This case demonstrates not so much the application of new law as the inapplicability of formerly applicable statute law. The Supreme Court of the Netherlands, in its decision of 8 June 1173 (see note 58), held that the law applicable to an employee of American Express in respect of the last six years of his employment, when he was in charge of European operations from a base in the Netherlands, was not the same as that which had been applicable earlier.

[70] See for example a decision of the Court of Cassation of 5 November 1979 (*J. Trib. Travail*, 1981, pp. 71-72).

[71] See A. Lyon-Caen, op. cit. in note 68, at pp. 749-750, and a decision of the District Court of Amsterdam of 14 December 1977 (*N.J.*, 1978, No. 426).

[72] However, in a decision of 5 May 1955 the Federal Labour Court stated that there was no general principle that managerial staff necessarily had a contract subject to the law of the head office of the undertaking.

[73] See in particular the decisions of the Court of Appeal in *Wilson* v. *Maynard Ship-building*, [1978] I.C.R. 376, and in *Ahmed* v. *Janata Bank*, [1981] *Industr. Rel. Law Rep.* 457.

[74] For certain cases (for instance if the work is carried out mainly in the country in which the worker is resident) the law of that country is preferred by the European Convention on Social Security, EEC Regulation 1408/71 and the Convention of the African and Mauritian Common Organisation.

[75] See Goldschmidt, op. cit. in note 55.

[76] See note 58.

[77] See note 41.

[78] ILO: *Report of the Committee of Experts on the Application of Conventions and Recommendations*, Report III (Part IV), International Labour Conference, 40th Session, Geneva, 1957, p. 41.

[79] See for instance article 9 of the Italian Navigation Code of 1942; article 5 of the French Seamen's Code of 1926 (*L.S.* 1977, Fr. 1); section 1 of the Seamen's Act of 1957 of the Federal Republic of Germany (*L.S.* 1957, Ger. F.R. 4).

[80] Argentina: decision of the Labour Court of Appeals of Buenos Aires of 30 June 1949 (however, a special rule, using the place of conclusion of the contract, has sometimes been applied to contracts for one round trip under which the seafarer has to be returned to that place; decision of the same court of 17 March 1955 and of the National Labour Court of 13 June 1957); all cited in Goldschmidt, op. cit. in note 55. Federal Republic of Germany: decisions of the Federal Labour Court of 30 May 1963 (*A.P.*, Case No. 7 under "IPR Arbeitsrecht") and 26 September 1978 (cited in Reithmann, op. cit. in note 34); in a decision of 29 November 1973 (No. 8/2 RU 158/72) the Federal Social Court held the social security law of the Federal Republic to be mandatorily applicable on ships flying its flag, although in the case before it the contracts of the crew were (by party choice?) subject to Pakistani law. Madagascar: Court of Appeal of Antananarivo, 5 December 1968 (*Travail et prof. d'outre-mer*, 2 Dec. 1969, p. 5974). United States: decisions of the Supreme Court of 25 May 1953 (*Lauritzen* v. *Larsen*, 345 U.S. 571) and of 18 February 1963 (*McCulloch* v. *Sociedad Nacional de Marineros de Honduras*, 372 U.S. 10), as well as a number of decisions of lower courts regarding claims to wages.

[81] *D° del trabajo*, 1971, p. 317.

[82] *IPRspr.*, 1974, No. 43.

[83] See F. Leffler: "Das Recht der Flagge im internationalen Seearbeitsrecht", in *Recht der Arbeit* (Munich), 1978, pp. 97-101.

[84] See B. A. Hepple: "Conflict of laws in employment relationships within the E.E.C.", in K. Lipstein (ed.): *Harmonisation of private international law by the E.E.C.* (London, 1978).

[85] *Clunet*, 1957, pp. 162 ff.

[86] See Fragistas in *RabelsZ.*, 1955, p. 147.

[87] 389 U.S. 306 (*Hellenic Lines* v. *Rhoditis*).

[88] *A.P.*, Case No. 19 under "IPR Arbeitsrecht".

[89] See for instance the Norwegian Regulations of 21 October 1976 concerning the application of the Seamen's Act to persons employed on board (mobile) oil drilling vessels or platforms and the exclusion of such mobile structures from the Royal Decree of 24 June 1977 relating to the protection of workers in connection with the exploration for and exploitation of submarine natural resources; J. Kitchen: *Labour law and offshore oil* (London, 1977) as regards Netherlands and British law; and G. J. Timagenis: "The legal status of engines operating at sea other than ships", in *Rev. hell. droit int.*, 1979, pp. 112 ff., for Greek law.

[90] An exception is L. Garofalo: "Disciplina internazional-privatistica e prassi contratuale dei rapporti di lavoro in stato di *insulation*", in *Riv. dir. int. priv. proc.*, 1976, pp. 756-781.

[91] In a decision of 1978 (*Claisse* v. *Keydril Ltd.*, [1978] I.C.R. 812), the British Employment Appeals Tribunal considered that a worker employed on a North Sea rig was not "ordinarily working" in Great Britain for the purpose of the application of legislation on dismissal. However, the decision was criticised by the Master of the Rolls in a later case (*Todd* v. *British Midland Airways*, [1978] I.C.R. 959) on the ground that the British home port should have been regarded as the worker's "base". In a decision of 1982, the National Labour Court of Israel applied Israeli law, by reference to the implied intention of the parties, to employment in

the Gulf of Suez on a rig registered in Panama of an Israeli citizen by the Israeli subsidiary of a United States corporation. The Court found expressly that the rig was not a vessel subject to legislation concerning seamen.

[92] The preference so given, which is expressly reserved by article 7, paragraph 2, of the E.E.C. Convention on the Law Applicable to Contractual Obligations, may itself be regarded as a rule of private international law. See for instance L. Schwander: Lois d'application immédiate, *Sonderanknüpfung, IPR Sachnormen und andere Ausnahmen von der gewöhnlichen Anknüpfung im internationalen Privatrecht* (Zurich, 1975).

[93] *L.S.* 1976, Arg. 1. It is likely that the general rules of the Civil Code would produce an analogous result.

[94] United Republic of Cameroon, Labour Code (*L.S.* 1974, Cam. 1), section 29; Gabon, Labour Code (*L.S.* 1978, Gab. 1), section 21; Ivory Coast, Labour Code (*L.S.* 1964, I.C. 1), section 29; Madagascar, Labour Code (*L.S.* 1975, Mad. 1), section 21; Mauritania, Labour Code (*L.S.* 1963, Mau. 1), section 6; Senegal, Labour Code (*L.S.* 1962, Sen. 2 B), section 32.

[95] *L.S.* 1978, Ec. 1.

[96] *L.S.* 1980, U.A.E. 1.

[97] *L.S.* 1981, Ang. 1.

[98] *L.S.* 1970, Iraq 1.

[99] See the sources cited in note 38.

[100] *L.S.* 1969, Mex. 1, section 5.

[101] *L.S.* 1971, Pan. 1, section 2.

[102] See in particular P. Francescakis: "Lois d'application immédiate et droit du travail", in *Rev. crit.*, 1974, pp. 273-296; J. Piron: "Eléments de réflexion pour la solution des conflits de lois en matière de droit du travail", in *Droit social*, 1966, pp. 212 ff.; F. Pocar: "Norme di applicazione necessaria e conflitti di leggi in tema di rapporti di lavoro", in *Riv. dir. int. priv. proc.*, 1967, pp. 734-744; P. Calleri: "Sulle norme di applicazione necessaria in materia di lavoro", in *Riv. dir. int.*, 1970, pp. 551 ff.

[103] As has been seen, some British legislation prohibiting discrimination on grounds of sex is imperative. In the United States, a decision of the Supreme Court of 15 June 1982 (28 *F.E.P. Cases*, pp. 1753-1759) suggests that though wholly owned subsidiaries of foreign companies are obliged to comply with such legislation if they are incorporated in the United States, commercial treaties may exempt branches of foreign companies which are not independent. Special problems may arise in countries in which principles of equal treatment are contained exclusively in the Constitution; in particular, it may not be clear in such cases whether these principles create direct rights and obligations for individuals.

[104] Com (75) 653 final.

[105] *Rev. crit.*, 1974, p. 350.

[106] *Arbeitsrecht in Stichworten*, 1975, p. 100 (or *A.P.*, Case No. 1 under section 106 of the Works Constitution Act (BVG)), and *A.P.*, Case No. 13 under "IPR Arbeitsrecht".

[107] Employment Protection (Consolidation) Act, 1978. Writers in the Federal Republic of Germany have also favoured the mandatory application of legal provisions concerning payments for periods not worked. See for instance R. Birk: "Lohnfortzahlungsgesetz und Auslandsbeziehungen", in *Der Betrieb*, 1973, p. 1551.

[108] France: Paris Court of Appeal, 4 July 1975 (*Rev. crit.*, 1976, pp. 485 ff.); Federal Republic of Germany: Federal Labour Court, 27 August 1964 (*A.P.*, Case No. 9 under "IPR Arbeitsrecht").

[109] Commercial Court, Brussels, 3 March 1970 (*Clunet*, 1975, p. 357).

[110] *Pasicrisie belge*, 1976, I, p. 1038.

[111] *J. Trib. Travail*, 1977, pp. 33-36.

[112] ibid., 1979, pp. 12-14.

[113] Court of Cassation, 7 December 1978, *J.C.P.*, 1979, IV, No. 55.

[114] Decision of Federal Labour Court of 10 April 1975 cited in note 41.

[115] Decision of Federal Labour Court of 9 November 1977 (*A.P.*, Case No. 13 under "IPR Arbeitsrecht").

[116] See in particular decisions of the Tribunal of Milan of 26 September 1968 (*Riv. dir. int.*, 1970, pp. 334 ff.), and of 28 February 1974 (*Riv. dir. int. priv. proc.*, 1976, p. 341, upheld

on appeal, ibid., p. 367). In the latter decision it was also held that provisions on a thirteenth month of salary were not mandatory. A different view on all three points was taken by the court of first instance of Genoa on 30 April 1980 (ibid., 1980, p. 458).

[117] See for instance a decision of the Supreme Court of 8 January 1971 (*Clunet*, 1978, pp. 335-336).

[118] For instance, in a decision of 29 November 1973 the Federal Social Court of the Federal Republic of Germany held that its social security legislation applied mandatorily on board ships flying the flag of the Federal Republic, as part of its territory in international law, even though the contracts of the crew were governed by Pakistani law (Case No. 8/2/RU 158/72).

[119] As will be seen in Chapter III, the law of the place where the injury is suffered has a major claim to be considered the applicable law for the purpose of damages. Quite apart from the special status of ships, however, courts appear to have hesitated on the question whether that law decides the validity of contractual clauses limiting liability in a relation subject to a different law.

[120] *Brodin* v. *A/R Seljan*, 1973 S.L.T. 198. For a discussion of that case see J. M. Thomson: "International employment contracts: The Scottish approach", in *Int. Compar. Law Q.*, 1974, p. 458. The case can also be seen as an example of the refusal to apply foreign law as contrary to local public policy (see section D of the present chapter).

[121] *Hellenic Lines* v. *Rhoditis*, 389 U.S. 306.

[122] *Romero* v. *International Terminal Operating Co.*, 358 U.S. 354 (1959).

[123] 372 U.S.10.

[124] A number of West European countries have, by an informal agreement among themselves, worked out in detail the manner of so doing.

[125] ILO: *Record of Proceedings*, International Labour Conference, 62nd Session, Geneva, 1976, p. 193.

[126] Case No. 1402/1980. Other elements were conclusion of the contract in the Netherlands, instructions and wage payments from there, and admission to the Netherlands labour market after dismissal. For earlier decisions on the applicability of the decree to work on the Netherlands part of the continental shelf, see *Neth. Yearb. Int. Law*, 1982, pp. 394-395.

[127] *L.S.* 1980, Sp. 1.

[128] *L.S.* 1973, Ven. 1.

[129] *Yugoslav Law*, 1979, No. 3, pp. 67-69.

[130] 24 *F.E.P. Cases* 747. The decision was set aside on appeal, but not on this issue (28 *F.E.P. Cases* 727). As indicated above, British mandatory legislation is not strictly territorial. The possibility of wider extraterritorial reach is examined in M. Forde: "Transnational employment and employment protection", in *Industr. Law J.*, 1978, pp. 228-238.

[131] See F. Morgenstern and B. Knapp: "Multinational enterprises and the extraterritorial application of labour law", in *Int. Compar. Law Q.*, 1978, pp. 769-793; R. Birk: "Multinational corporations and international labour law", in *International law problems of multinational corporations* (Heidelberg, 1978); and G. Z. Northstein and J. P. Ayres: "The multinational corporation and the extraterritorial application of the Labor-Management Relations Act", in *Cornell Int. Law J.*, Vol. 10, pp. 1-58.

[132] See in particular P. Mayer: "Les lois de police étrangères", in *Clunet*, 1981, pp. 277-345; and K. Lipstein: "Inherent limitations in statutes and the conflict of laws", in *Int. Compar. Law Q.*, 1977, pp. 884 ff.

[133] Of United States case law it has been said that "the results are consistent enough to warrant the generalisation that a law restrictive of freedom of contract, designed to protect an economically weaker party, will almost invariably be applied if the weaker party's home at the time of contracting was in the state with the protective law, or if he was to perform the contract there" (Joost Blom in *Can. Yearb. Int. Law*, 1979, at p. 240). However, in the employment cases summarised in the *Restatement in the Courts* published from time to time by the American Law Institute it is also "almost invariably" the law of the forum which is applied on that basis.

[134] See for instance a decision of the Labour Court of Huy of 7 November 1980, in *J. Trib. Travail*, 1981, p. 37.

[135] In its decision of 31 May 1972 (see note 51), the Court of Cassation considered the law of the place of performance to be applicable in so far as it related to "national public policy,

particularly in respect of the organisation and administrative regulation of labour matters", but applied the chosen (French) law as more favourable to the employee. In a decision of 29 January 1975 (*Clunet*, 1976, pp. 144-145) the same court upheld a decision to give effect in France to a Senegalese judgement applying Senegalese mandatory law to a contract of employment originally made subject to French law but performed in Senegal; however, it did so on the ground that the parties, having been made aware of the requirements of Senegalese law, had implicitly accepted it.

[136] *Rev. crit.*, 1967, p. 522. The decision did not relate to labour matters. In France, the Paris Court of Appeal, in its decision of 4 July 1975 (see note 65) expressed respect for the applicability of the law of the place of work in the same terms as the Court of Cassation in its decision of 31 May 1972 cited in the preceding note, in a case in which French law was not the chosen law but the law otherwise applicable. Again, however, French law was found to be more favourable. See also article 7 of the 1971 resolution of the Institute of International Law on conflicts of laws in the field of labour law.

[137] Argentina: M. L. Deveali, in *D° del trabajo*, 1952, p. 65; Belgium: V. Vannes, in *J. Trib. Travail*, 1981, at p. 239; Brazil, France, Great Britain and Italy: the sources cited in note 25.

[138] For instance, the ILO Migration for Employment Convention (Revised), 1949, provides for treatment "no less favourable" than that applied to nationals.

[139] See note 41.

[140] See for instance decisions of the Tribunal of Milan of 26 September 1968 and 28 February 1974, cited in note 116. In the decision referred to in the preceding note, the Federal Labour Court of the Federal Republic of Germany spoke of an effect "so contrary to the line of thought underlying the German provisions in the matter that it is felt by [the Court] to be wholly unacceptable".

[141] Tribunal of Genoa, 6 November 1974 (*Riv. dir. int. priv. proc.*, 1975, p. 131).

[142] Cases cited in F. Gamillscheg: *Internationales Arbeitsrecht* (Tübingen, 1959), at p. 71.

[143] For instance *Blalock* v. *Perfect Subscription Co.*, 458 F. Supp. 123 (1978), upheld 599 F. 2d 743 (1979), where an anti-competition covenant in a contract subject to Pennsylvania law was denied enforcement in Alabama as contrary to public policy.

[144] See Gamillscheg, op. cit. in note 142, at p. 72.

[145] A. Vasquez Vialard (ed.): *Tratado de derecho del trabajo* (Buenos Aires, 1982), Vol. II, Ch. VII (by E. L. Fermé), p. 903.

[146] Civil Code, articles 14 and 15.

[147] Central African Republic, Law No. 65-71 (of 3 June 1965), articles 32 and 33; Gabon, introductory part of Civil Code, article 27; Guinea, Law No. 52-62 (of 14 April 1962), articles 4 and 5.

[148] G. M. C. Russomano: *Direito internacional privado do trabalho* (Rio de Janeiro, 2nd ed., 1979), pp. 203 ff.

[149] Code of Civil Procedure, section 184.

[150] Article 638 of the Belgian Code of Civil Procedure, article 18 (2) of the Italian code and article 126 (3) of that of the Netherlands.

[151] See for instance *Clunet*, 1973, pp. 800 ff., for decisions of the Spanish Supreme Court of 1966 and 1968.

[152] Law on Jurisdiction, article 66.

[153] Code of Civil Procedure, articles 12-13.

[154] L. A. Lunz: *Internationaler Zivilprozess* (Berlin, 1968), at p. 38.

[155] Code of Civil Procedure, article 126 (1).

[156] Act regarding judicial procedure, article 17.

[157] Federal Constitution, article 59.

[158] Lunz, op. cit. in note 154, pp. 44 ff., or the Russian original published in Moscow in 1966.

[159] See for instance article 125 (*b*) of the Netherlands Code of Civil Procedure. See also article 112 of the Swiss draft legislation on private international law. By a decision of 12 June 1979 (*Riv. dir. int. priv. proc.*, 1980, p. 260), the full bench of the Italian Court of Cassation held that there was jurisdiction, on the basis of the general provision of the Code of Civil

Procedure regarding the place of performance of a contract, with respect to an employment relation with a United States company, where the work was carried out in Italy. A similar view was taken by the Spanish Supreme Court in a decision of 22 June 1964 (*Clunet*, 1973, p. 800).

[160] *Financial Times*, 12 May 1980, p. 25.

[161] *MacShannon* v. *Rockware Glass Co.* [1978] A.C. 795.

[162] *Clunet*, 1971, pp. 792 ff. The Convention came into force for the original six Members of the EEC in 1973. New Members have undertaken to accede to the Convention, which was modified somewhat in 1978 (*Clunet*, 1979, pp. 204-217) to facilitate the accession of Denmark, Ireland and the United Kingdom.

[163] This applies only to defendants domiciled within the EEC. The concept of domicil is not defined.

[164] There are special provisions on insurance and on hire-purchase agreements. Special provisions for contracts of employment were considered, but finally not included. For a criticism of this omission see A. Huet in *Clunet*, 1980, p. 429, and L. Mari: "Rapporti di lavoro, principi costituzionali e deroga alla giurisdizione secondo la Convenzione di Bruxelles del 1968", in *Riv. dir. int. priv. proc.*, 1981, pp. 51-84. It should be noted that the provisions of the Convention do not necessarily solve all problems. Court cases have already shown that there may be argument as to where the contract obligation is performed. In a case before the Court of Appeal of Angers, France, in January 1980 (*Rev. crit.*, 1981, pp. 118 ff.), the question arose whether the determining factor was the fact that the employee worked in France or the fact that the indemnities sought were payable by the employer in Belgium. The Court assumed jurisdiction on the ground that there had been non-performance of obligations under a contract which was governed by French law.

[165] For instance, the list of the subjects covered in treaties on judicial assistance between the various socialist countries given in Lunz, op. cit. in note 154 is essentially limited to family law.

[166] *Rev. crit.*, 1978, pp. 166-167, with a note by H. Battifol.

[167] *Riv. dir. int. priv. proc.*, 1980, p. 82.

[168] In particular Mari, op. cit. in note 164.

[169] In addition to the publications cited in note 164, see G. Beitzke: "Gerichtsstandsklauseln in auslandsbezogenen Dienst- und Arbeitsverträgen", in *R.I.W./A.W.D.*, 1976, pp. 7 ff.; F. Pocar: "Jurisdiction and the enforcement of judgments under the E.E.C. Convention of 1968", in *RabelsZ.*, 1978, pp. 405 ff.; and J. Vincent: "Quelques observations sur les conflits de juridictions en matière de contrat de travail", in *Etudes de droit du travail offertes à André Brun* (Paris, 1974), pp. 603-617.

[170] As in the case of other legislation which is imperative internally, the question of the extent to which it is also mandatory in international situations is an open one. In some cases (e.g. of some French-speaking African countries) the provisions in question are included in texts which are clearly applicable also to international relations.

[171] *Clunet*, 1980, p. 429.

[172] *Riv. dir. int. priv. proc.*, 1980, p. 82; see also a decision of the Court of Appeal of Aix-en-Provence of 10 May 1974 (*Rev. crit.*, 1974, p. 548).

[173] *Clunet*, 1975, p. 360. By decision of 7 February 1980 (*J. Trib. Travail*, 1982, pp. 205-206) the Labour Court of Appeal of Antwerp held valid a clause in a contract of employment vesting jurisdiction in the courts of the Netherlands without reference to a treaty.

[174] Decisions of the Court of Cassation (Ch. mixte) of 28 June 1974 (*J.C.P.*, 1974, II, No. 17881) and (Ch. civ.) of 29 January 1975 (*Clunet*, 1976, pp. 145-146), as well as a decision of the Court of Appeal of Rennes of 8 December 1977 (ibid., 1978, pp. 885 ff.). The last-mentioned case dealt with a point left open by the earlier decisions, namely whether the conclusion of the contract in France was sufficient to exclude the possibility of choice.

[175] Decisions of 20 July 1970 (*A.P.*, Case No. 4 under section 38 of the Rules of Civil Procedure (ZPO)) and 5 September 1972 (*A.P.*, Case No. 159 under section 242 of the Civil Code (BGB) "Ruhegehalt").

[176] *A.P.*, Case No. 8 under section 38 of ZPO.

[177] *Int. Labour Law Rep.*, Vol. 3, Swe 4.

ESTABLISHMENT, CONDITIONS AND TERMINATION OF THE INTERNATIONAL EMPLOYMENT RELATION

The legal principles discussed in Chapter II have practical implications, discussed in the present chapter, for the establishment, conditions and termination of the international employment relation.[1]

A. ESTABLISHMENT OF THE EMPLOYMENT RELATION

Determination of the existence of an employment relation presupposes the determination of the parties to that relation; in the case of a multi-national group of companies, however, it may be difficult to decide which is the employer. For the relation to come into existence it is further necessary that the parties should have the capacity in law to commit themselves; that legal requirements regarding the formalities to be completed have been met; and that the arrangements made are valid, in particular in the sense of not violating legal prohibitions.

The employer

Three main types of situations raise questions regarding the identity of the employer. One is that of the movement of the employee from one legally independent company to another within a group. Personnel leasing raises some analogous questions and can accordingly be assimilated to this type of situation. A second is that of a change in the ownership of the employing undertaking as a result of mergers, take-overs and other forms of transfer. The third (and most difficult) is that of an employment relation within a group of companies which is ambiguous from its inception; this may be because the hiring is done by a company which does nothing but exercise personnel functions for the group, or because, although the employee is at all times in the service of a particular subsidiary, certain powers in relation to him are exercised by the parent company or by another subsidiary.

. The first problem which arises when any of these situations concerns more than one country is which law to apply to the determination of the employer. It has long been necessary to distinguish employment from other relationships with agents, independent contractors and family members, and a variety of tests (such as control over the work, or payment of wages) evolved for this purpose are also used singly or in combination to define the employer. The approaches of different countries to this question can produce different results.

Early in the 1970s the view was taken by some that the issue had to be decided by reference to the law governing the employment relation.[2] They reasoned on the assumption that within a group of companies there is a *prima facie* employment relation with the member of the group in the activities of which the employee participates, and that what is at issue is to determine, in the light of the law governing that relation, whether the employee has any rights against another member of the group, or against the group as a whole – to "pierce the veil" of the internal group arrangements. However, as was pointed out by others, even at that time,[3] the question of who is the real employer may affect the determination of the law applicable to the individual employment relation – particularly, though not exclusively, where tests such as the "proper law" or the *Schwerpunkt* of the relation are applied. A striking, though by no means isolated, example is provided by a decision of 4 June 1980[4] of the Court of Appeal of Aix-en-Provence, in France, which found that the contract regarding an employment relation with the French subsidiary of a United States corporation for which the plaintiff last worked had been a "façade", that the real relation was with the parent company in the United States and that United States law applied to that relation. It has also been pointed out that the definition of the employing undertaking may have a bearing on collective labour relations, which should not be dependent on the law applicable to an individual contract.[5] While, therefore, the *prima facie* employment relation may be and appears in practice to be the starting-point for the settlement of certain claims – in particular those involving the taking into account, for seniority or indemnities, of successive employment with different members of the same group of companies (see section C below) – it cannot as readily serve as the basis for a more general determination of the parties to the employment relation.

The main other possibility is to use the law of the "forum". This is tantamount to making the question one of classification, to be decided before a choice of law can be made. Traditionally, the question whether there was an employment relation (as opposed to some other form of legal relationship) was considered to be a matter of classification, to be decided by reference to the concepts of the private international law of the forum.[6] Since the identification of the parties is a step towards the finding that there is an employment relation, a number of authors have taken the view that this problem must be treated in the same manner.[7] The case law on this subject is unhelpful in the sense that courts do not appear to have addressed themselves directly to this question and that the law of the forum and of the *prima facie* employment relation often coincide; what can be said, however, is that courts do not seem to have ever applied to the question the concepts of a law that was not, inter alia, that of the forum.[8]

The inherent complexity of the question of the determination of the employer in any case calls for two additional comments. First, it is becoming increasingly accepted that there can be a plurality of employers. A triangular relation, with one undertaking normally responsible for the supervision of the work and for carrying out the obligations of the employer at the workplace and a second responsible for tenure of employment, for wages and for social security, is now recognised in a number of countries as typical of personnel leasing. Within groups of companies, also, a division of the responsibilities of the employer between two or more entities is not uncommon: a recent study of the practice of a number of companies incorporated in the Federal Republic of Germany in the detachment and transfer of workers abroad showed that in a number of cases there was a double relation;[9] a similar conclusion has been derived from case law in France.[10] In a decision of 21 December 1982 the District Court of Haarlem in the Netherlands found that although a company incorporated in the Federal Republic of Germany was given as the employer in the contract of a Chilean working offshore, the worker's recruitment, normal wage payments and dismissal were handled by a sister company incorporated in the Netherlands; the Court considered that since the companies acted "interchangeably" as the employer, the one incorporated in the Netherlands could not argue, in defence against a claim by the worker, that the one incorporated in the Federal Republic of Germany should have been sued.[11]

Secondly, the identification of the employer or employers by no means exhausts the implications which the existence of a group of companies may have in labour law or private international law; this is particularly so because in the present state of the law a group as such does not normally have the legal standing to be formally regarded as the employer. One aspect of this question is the possible liability of a parent company for the debts of a subsidiary to its employees. In two countries internal law provides for such liability: section 2 (2) of the Brazilian Consolidated Labour Laws, and section 31 of the Argentinian Consolidated Rules governing Contracts of Employment. Internationally, the matter came before the Organisation for Economic Co-operation and Development in 1977, in the *Badger* case, as an issue of interpretation of the provision of its guidelines on multinational enterprises stating that the guidelines are addressed to the various entities within the enterprise according to the actual distribution of responsibilities among them, on the understanding that they will co-operate and provide assistance to one another as necessary to facilitate observance of the guidelines. While the specific case was settled on the basis of payment by the parent company of the debts of its fully owned subsidiary, the 1979 review of the guidelines makes clear (in paragraph 42) that the provision relied on cannot be seen in a legal framework and does not imply an unqualified principle of parent company responsibility; the comment is added that the question of financial responsibility could arise as a matter of good management practice in particular circumstances. Other aspects of intra-group relations will be examined below in connection with substantive issues of the employment relation.

The question of the law applicable to the effects of mergers, take-overs and other transfers of the employing undertaking is distinct from that considered hitherto. What is at issue here is which law decides whether an existing employment relation is mandatorily transferred to the new owner of the undertaking if the former employer ceases to exist as such (although this is not always the result when a formerly independent undertaking joins a group). It has been suggested that the most appropriate law to determine that issue is the law of the place where the undertaking which has changed hands is situated; [12] if that undertaking itself has branches or subsidiaries in more than one country, it may be that the law of the place of establishment of each needs to decide. Within the European Communities an attempt has been made to eliminate possible conflicts of laws on the subject by a harmonisation of substantive law. A directive of 14 February 1977 on the safeguarding of employees' rights in the event of transfer of undertakings, businesses or parts of businesses [13] provides that the rights and obligations of the former employer pass to the new, and that transfer is not itself a ground for termination of employment. The directive applies to any undertaking, business or part of business within the territorial scope of the Treaty of Rome, and thus seems to support the view that the place of the undertaking or of a part thereof determines the applicable law, even in relation to third States. This is made very clear by the British regulations of 1981 giving effect to the directive: they specify that they apply irrespective of the law governing the transfer and that governing the employment relation.

A further issue is that of the effect of the identification of the employer on the law applicable to the employment relation. Some of the legislation and case law cited in Chapter II, section B, with reference to transfers and detachment of employees and to personnel leasing, shows an inter-relation between the tests used to determine, on the one hand, who is the employer and, on the other hand, what law is applicable to the employment relation: the overall power of direction plays a key role in both. There may be a similar convergence in some of the cases in which the employment relation within a group of companies is ambiguous from its inception. On the other hand, in the case of transfers of undertakings or parts thereof, the problem, for the question of applicable law as for that of survival of the existing employment relation, is whether the mere fact of a change in employer need involve a change in the legal position of the employee. The original draft of the above-cited directive of the European Communities [14] included an article expressly providing that the law applicable to employment relations prior to the transfers remained applicable; it reserved the situation of a lawful transfer to work in another country or of an agreed change in applicable law, while safeguarding substantive contractual rights even in such a case. The article was dropped in the final text, apparently so as to avoid any possible conflict with the draft regulation specifically concerned with the law applicable to employment relations.[15] However, the substantive provisions which are to be embodied in the law of the countries concerned – i.e. the maintenance of existing rights and obligations – would seem to imply that the law applicable to the employment relation will not change merely as a result of the fact that the undertaking has been transferred to a new owner.

Capacity

In labour law the most common example of limitations on the capacity to conclude a contract relates to the employment or apprenticeship contracts of minors. What is at issue as regards the minor is not the prohibition of work under a certain age (which will be considered below), but the ability to decide to enter employment: very widely the consent of parent or guardian is a prerequisite;[16] however, it is so in different degrees (for instance, in some countries it must be express, in some it may be tacit, in yet others it is not necessary if the young person, with the tacit consent of parent or guardian, lives independently). Conversely, there may be limitations on the capacity of an employer to accept apprentices.[17] Given the national differences in the matter, the question of the applicable law arises.

Some countries have a special rule for determining the law which governs the capacity to enter into an employment relation. Thus section 27 (3) of the Act of 1975 determining applicable law of the German Democratic Republic provides that the law governing the employment relation by virtue of paragraphs 1 and 2 of that section (i.e. the law of the place of the employer's principal place of business or the law of the place of work if it is also the employee's habitual place of residence) also governs the capacity to enter into a contract of employment.[18] In other countries the matter is covered by the general rules of private international law relating to the capacity to perform legal acts.[19] These rules quite commonly refer to the "personal law", which may be, in the case of individuals, the law of their nationality or of their domicil and, in the case of corporate bodies, the law of the country of their incorporation or of their place of business.

For employment relations as for other types of contract it is desirable that rules regarding capacity should not create excessive barriers to agreement. The need to obtain information regarding the personal law of prospective employees might be such a barrier. A number of countries provide that it is sufficient, for a contract entered into in their territory, that the parties satisfy the requirements regarding capacity in force in that territory.[20] Similarly, the EEC Convention on the Law Applicable to Contractual Obligations provides, in article 11, that "in a contract concluded between persons who are in the same country, a natural person who would have capacity under the law of that country may invoke his incapacity resulting from another law only if the other party to the contract was aware of this incapacity at the time of the conclusion of the contract or was not aware thereof as a result of negligence". The Swiss Bill, as submitted to Parliament, has a provision analogous to that of the EEC. Where provisions of this kind are in force, a contract will be regarded as validly concluded if the individual concerned has the necessary capacity either under his personal law or under the law of the place of conclusion (particularly when the latter is also the law of the forum). They must be distinguished from the (relatively rare) cases in which reference to the law of the place of conclusion is the sole rule of private international law,[21] and those in which the requirements of the personal law and of the law of the place of conclusion are cumulative in the sense that capacity under the personal law does not suffice if there is no capacity under the law of the place of conclusion.[22]

As regards the employer, limitations on his capacity to enter into contracts of apprenticeship would appear to be so linked with the policies of the country in which the contract is concluded or, where it is different, of the country in which the contract is to be performed, that it would seem to be the law of that country rather than the personal law of the employer which is determining. On this point, however, no guidance is to be obtained from court decisions or other sources.

Formalities

The main formal requirement in labour law is that certain types or particular provisions of contracts of employment should be in writing. Such a requirement is widespread, but its object varies. In some countries all contracts of employment must be in writing;[23] in others, contracts for longer than a specified period;[24] in some, contracts for a specified time,[25] or for work remunerated by the piece or by the task,[26] or contracts for part-time work[27] or home work.[28] The consequences of the failure to comply with the requirement also differ: in some countries the validity of the contract is affected and the employer cannot rely on its terms although the employee's rights are safeguarded to varying degrees;[29] the counterpart of failure to put fixed-term contracts into written form is often the transformation of the contract into one for an unlimited period of time;[30] in yet other cases, the contract is unaffected but the employer is subject to penalties.[31] Given all these divergences, it is again important to know which law applies.

The rules of private international law relating to contracts generally tend to be so conceived as to reduce to a minimum the number of cases in which failure to meet formal requirements makes the agreement of the parties ineffective. They frequently provide that it is sufficient if the agreement meets legal provisions regarding form of either the place of conclusion of the contract or of the law which is to govern it.[32] In some cases there are even additional possibilities, such as meeting the requirements of the law of common nationality or domicil.[33] The EEC Convention on the Law Applicable to Contractual Obligations gives the following possibilities: the law which is to govern the contract and, as regards a contract concluded by persons in the same country, that of the place of its conclusion or, as regards a contract concluded by persons in different countries, that of one of those countries. A number of other countries use the place of conclusion of the contract as the test,[34] which allows an "easy" country to be chosen for negotiating the contract; furthermore, Argentina, for instance, applies the principle that, where a contract is concluded between parties in two different countries, the law most favourable to the validity of the contract is regarded as that of the place of conclusion.

As regards contracts of employment the question arises whether the protective purpose of the formal requirements should not override the principle of favouring agreement; as in the case of choice of law by the parties, we have the problem of the "weaker party". The protective purpose can prevail in a number of ways. First, in two countries (the German Democratic Republic and Hungary) there are specific legal provisions concerning contracts of employment; matters of form are subject to the law applicable, under the terms of that legislation, to the employment relation. Secondly, under the general rule of the Bustamante Code that the requirements as to form of the law of the place of conclusion and the law of the place of performance are not alternatives but are cumulative, the governments of countries like Brazil apply the formal requirements of their own internal law to contracts of employment to be performed there even if they have been concluded elsewhere, in cases in which those internal requirements are more stringent than those of the internal law of the place of conclusion.[35] Thirdly, some countries, such as Czechoslovakia and Portugal, qualify their general, liberal rule by a proviso that compliance with the law of the place of conclusion is not sufficient if the requirements of the law which is to govern the contract are a condition of the contract's validity. Finally, and perhaps of most general application, there is the possibility that the provisions in question are mandatory in the sense of overriding the general rules of private international law (see Chapter II, section C), either at the place of conclusion [36] or at the place of performance of the employment relation.

Compliance with substantive legal requirements

Various legal prescriptions and prohibitions have to be complied with if a contract of employment is to be valid and enforceable. Two examples, which call for somewhat different treatment in private international law, will be considered here. One is that of the minimum age for admission to employment; in national legislation it varies from 12 to 18, and there remain countries which have no minimum at all. The other example is the legislative prohibition or regulation of certain types of placement in employment (for instance, placement by private agencies, and recruitment and placement of aliens) and of personnel leasing.

As was indicated in Chapter II, section C, legislation such as that concerning the minimum age for admission to employment is generally regarded as mandatory at the place at which the work is to be performed; there is thus no doubt that the law of that place must be complied with.[37] However, the statement of that fact does not exhaust the subject: there remains the question whether any other law applies to the extent that its requirements are more stringent than those of the place of work. Under general rules of private international law, the validity of a contract as regards substance is often considered to be governed by the law which would be applicable to the contract once it was in existence.[38] As has been seen above, in the sphere of employment relations that law frequently coincides with the law applicable at the place of work, but it would seem reasonable to regard the law applicable to the contract as determining if it is different and more stringent. Such a conclusion is reinforced where, as under the EEC texts and some national legislation and case law on the subject, the mandatory legislation of the place of work is considered to provide a minimum of protection. On the other hand arguments made in favour of the applicability of a system of law which is neither that of the place of work nor that applicable to the contract would seem to be less convincing. It has been suggested that the country of the nationality or domicil of the young person concerned has an interest in the matter;[39] however, such authority as there is for the view is very old. It has also been suggested that this is an area in which the law of the head office of the parent company of a multinational group might appropriately be applied; significantly, the ILO Tripartite Declaration of Principles on Multinational Enterprises and Social Policy contains no mention of the subject.

Placement in employment and personnel leasing across frontiers affects the regulation of the labour market of two countries: that of recruitment and that of assignment. Since such regulation is normally a matter of public administration, the relevant legal provisions are likely to be mandatory in the sense of being applicable in preference to the general rules of private international law. Restrictions on placement or on personnel leasing in both the countries concerned accordingly have to be taken into account.[40] The non-respect of such restrictions does not necessarily affect the existence of the employment relation. In terms of the internal labour law of different countries, it is most likely to do so, on the one hand, in the case of the placement of aliens without a work permit, and, on the other, in the case of a contract with an unlicensed temporary work agency. In terms of private international law, it is most likely to do so where the restrictions are those of the country in which the work is to be performed, or where the restrictions are those of the country of recruitment and there is a continuing relationship with the sending agency in that country;[41] it is much more doubtful whether violation of restrictions in the country of recruitment makes invalid or unenforceable an employment relation agreed upon and implemented in another country the relevant requirements of which are met.[42] Some of the difficulties arising from the need to comply with two systems of control have been reduced within the European Communities by a decision of the Court of Justice of 18 January 1979;[43] it held that placement agencies whose principal place of business was in one member State could be made subject to the licensing system of another member State only if such subjection was objectively necessary; this was not so if the agency was licensed in the State in which it had its seat, on conditions comparable with those on which licences were issued in the other State concerned, and if its placement activities, wherever they took place, were subject to adequate supervision in its home State.

Consequences of invalidity of a contract of employment

When an employment relation has not validly come into existence, or is subsequently declared invalid, there may nevertheless be question of the rights of the worker, particularly if he has worked. National law frequently safeguards the position of the worker, but it does not always do so to the same extent: for instance, in some cases he can claim reasonable remuneration for work performed; in others he can rely on the terms of the otherwise ineffective contract.

The most widely followed rule regarding the law to be applied to the consequences of the invalidity of a contract is that of recourse to the law which would have governed the contract had it been valid (including, as appropriate, the law chosen by the parties).[44] There would appear to be no reason why this rule should not operate as regards employment relations, as is expressly specified, for example, in the legislative decree of 1979 in Hungary. At the same time, if the law in question is not that of the place at which work was carried out in pursuance of the invalid contract, it may be that the worker has some additional entitlements, at least on application to the authorities of the country in which he worked, under mandatory provisions of the law of that country.

B. TERMS AND CONDITIONS OF EMPLOYMENT

Terms and conditions of employment are the subject, par excellence, of the law applicable to the employment relation determined in accordance with the principles set out in Chapter II, sections A and B. The main areas in which that law may be overridden by the mandatory requirements of another legal system have been considered in Chapter II, section C. However, not only may it be useful to recall, subject by subject, what this may mean in practice; there are also complexities which cannot be altogether resolved on that basis alone.

Authority of the employer

The employer assigns the work. Many legal systems, however, place limitations on his authority to do so: he may not be able to oblige the employee to perform work other than that for which he was engaged, or to transfer him to a different location without his consent.[45]

It is generally considered that this is a matter governed by the law of the employment relation.[46] Court decisions have sometimes had that result, though the courts did not address themselves to the issue directly. For instance, the Labour Court of Appeal of Brussels was seized, in 1973, of a claim by the French manager of the Belgian branch of a French undertaking that a decision to transfer him to France was a breach of contract; it decided that it had no jurisdiction (the parties having contractually agreed on the competence of the French courts), but thus, in effect, left the matter to be settled by French law which it found to be the law applicable to the employment relation.[47] Similarly, in July 1981 the English Court of Appeal [48] decided that it had no jurisdiction to deal with a claim of unjustified dismissal from the manager of the branch of a Bangladesh bank who had refused re-transfer to Bangladesh; it did so by reference to the scope of the legislation governing its competence, but again by implication left the matter to the law governing the employment relation.

It may nevertheless be wrong to assume that this is universally true. For instance, in Argentina the pertinent provisions are contained in legislation which is applicable to all work performed within the country, regardless of the place of conclusion of the contract of employment. In the English case just cited the Court might have decided differently had it been able to find as a fact that the employee worked "ordinarily" in England. It is also conceivable that the authorities of a country may refuse to take account of the law governing the employment relation on the ground that a particular assignment permitted by that law is contrary to public policy.

Duties of care on the part of employer and employee

Different systems of law lay upon the employer, in varying degrees, a duty of care for the welfare of his employees. They require of the employee that he shall perform his work with due care. These reciprocal duties are governed by the law applicable to the employment relation, except in so far as certain aspects thereof (in particular regarding occupational safety and health) are dealt with by mandatory requirements of the law of the place of work (and that law is not the one applicable to the employment relation generally). Particular questions regarding the substance of the duties will be further examined below.

Of interest here are the possible results of failure to perform the duties. Generally breaches of mutual obligations may lead to a claim for compensation on the ground that the contract of employment has not been respected; such a claim is governed by the law applicable to the contract.

However, it may be possible as an alternative in some countries, or necessary in others, particularly where the failure causes physical injury or material damage, to bring the claim in tort, in civil liability. What is at issue is not legislation regarding compensation for employment injuries, even where it is based on the principle of employer's liability: such legislation belongs to the field of social security, which is not covered by the present survey. Several problems distinct from such legislation can arise: is there a claim under general rules regarding civil liability? Against whom can such a claim be made? Is such a claim precluded by legislative or contractual exemptions? What damage is actionable and what is the amount of compensation which can be recovered? These problems can derive from the actions and omissions of both employer and employee; all raise questions regarding which law is applicable.

The rules of private international law governing civil liability are quite different from those relating to contracts. Traditionally two systems of law play a major role: that of the place where the injury or damage was caused and that of the forum. In a number of countries the first alone is applicable [49] although there may be divergences of interpretation: is it the law of the place of the act or omission, or that of the place where the injury or damage was suffered, if the places are not the same? [50] In some other countries a combination is required: the claim must be possible both under the law of the place where the injury or damage was caused and under that of the forum.[51] The traditional approach has one major defect: the place where the injury or damage was caused may have no connection, other than a passing presence, with either the person causing the injury or damage or the victim, whereas another system of law may have a continuing connection with both; where the mate on a lorry engaged in international road transport is injured by the negligence of the driver, where both have the same nationality and domicil and are employed by an undertaking at that domicil, is it reasonable to apply the law of the country through which they happened to be passing at the time of the accident? [52] Palliatives have accordingly been sought.[53] It is provided in the legislation on private international law of a number of countries (the German Democratic Republic, Poland and Portugal) that the law of the common nationality or domicil of the parties concerned overrides any other law; this is also true of the Swiss Bill as submitted to Parliament. Under the Austrian federal law of 1978 there is a more flexible restriction on the applicability of the law of the place where the conduct causing the injury occurred: if the persons involved both have a stronger connection with the law of another State, that law is determining. In the United States a like approach is taken as regards personal injuries in the second *Restatement of the Law*. A similar trend emerges from recent decisions of English courts. The text which has become the EEC Convention on the Law Applicable to Contractual Obligations was originally intended to cover torts as well, and would have allowed the law of the place at which the injury was caused to be overriden by a preponderant different connection common to the parties; [54] however, it apparently proved more difficult to arrive at agreement in this area than in that of contracts. A treaty in a more specific field – the Hague Convention on the Law Applicable to Traffic Accidents, of 1971 – makes it possible for the law of the place at which the injury was caused to be left aside, in specified cases, in favour of the law of the country of registration of the vehicle. [55]

Treaties and draft treaties in the matter make the law agreed to be applicable govern all the problems which arise (other than those relating to insurance). This is not necessarily so under national rules of private international law. The law determined in accordance with the principles indicated in the foregoing paragraph relates primarily to the question whether there is a claim on the ground of liability for fault or for risk. It probably applies also to the question of who is liable, a question which in the employment relation bears mainly on the potential liability of the employer to employees or to third parties for the acts or omissions of his employees. [56] It does not necessarily apply to the compensation which may be obtained (for instance, to the question whether damages are payable for pain and suffering, and to the manner of assessment). A few countries provide expressly that compensation awarded in their courts must not exceed that obtainable under their law; [57] in other words, the law of the forum acts as a ceiling. Others apply the law of the forum as a matter of procedure or of public policy. [58] It has also been suggested that damages should be governed by the law of the domicil of the victim, so as to adjust them to his normal environment. [59] However that may be, the greatest difficulties are raised by statutory or contractual exemptions from liability.

Statutory exemptions from the liability of employer or fellow-employee for employment-related injuries are common in social security systems. [60] Their applicability should go hand in hand with that of the social security system of which they are a part. Some case law suggests that this may be so in practice. The Federal Labour Court of the Federal Republic of Germany held, in a decision of 30 October 1963, [61] that if a national of the Federal Republic was sent abroad by his employer and in the course of his work there caused an injury to a foreign employee of a foreign undertaking, reliance could not be placed on the exemption provisions of sections 898 and 899 of the Federal Insurance Law, irrespective of whether the foreign worker had similar insurance. Conversely, the Italian Court of Cassation held, on 29 July 1974, [62] in an action brought by the parents of an Italian worker killed during a short mission abroad, that Italian insurance applied and the exemption of the employer from civil suit was effective. In a number of recent cases in the United States claims in tort were decided (and rejected) by reference to the law under which workmen's compensation had been paid, although recovery might have been possible under the law of the place where the injury occurred. [63] At the same time, as indicated in section D of Chapter II above, the volume on conflict of laws in the second *Re-*

statement of the Law leaves open the question whether it would be possible to refuse to apply, by reference to public policy considerations, the exemption given in another state to persons who have not paid for insurance, i.e. to fellow-employees.

Contractual clauses, which appear to be widely used in multinational enterprises, are designed to permit claims exclusively under an agreed compensation scheme or under a specified system of law. The main problem they pose is whether their validity needs to be examined by reference to the law governing the contract in which they are included or by reference to that governing a claim in civil liability which they are designed to exclude. In the English case of *Sayers* v. *International Drilling Co. N.V.*[64] (already considered in Chapter II), the three judges of the Court of Appeal were divided on the approach to be taken: the majority treated the matter as a contractual problem and applied what they considered to be the law governing the contract; the third regarded the issue as one of tort, and arrived at the same substantive conclusion as the others only because he found the law of the seat of the undertaking, as the only common bond between employees the negligence of one of whom had injured another, to be the "proper law" of the tort.[65] In the Scottish case of *Brodin* v. *A/F Seljan*,[66] also mentioned earlier, a key factor was the fact that the injury was caused in Scottish territorial waters, although Scotland was also the forum and the mandatory nature of Scottish legislation (and perhaps public policy) certainly had a great deal to do with the result. In a field in which even the general rules are in a state of flux, a legal challenge to contractual clauses is likely to produce the most unforeseen results.

Remuneration

Remuneration is a contractual matter, *prima facie* subject to the law of the contract. However, as was indicated in Chapter II, section C, varying aspects of the subject may be governed by mandatory rules at the place where the work is performed. Such rules tend to deal with two main aspects of the subject.

The first is that of the amount of the remuneration. Statutory minimum wages are widely regarded as mandatory; this has, perhaps, only a limited effect in that the earnings of workers with contracts governed by foreign law are not usually at a level below the minimum of the place of work. Wage rates laid down by collective agreement could be more relevant; it has been suggested that any such rates that may have been made generally applicable should be regarded as mandatory, but this suggestion has not been followed in practice in all cases, as will be seen in Chapter IV. Certain bonuses, and in particular the "thirteenth month" of wages, are mandatory in some countries (e.g. Argentina)[67] but have been held not to be mandatory in others (e.g. Italy).[68] There may be mandatory provisions (e.g. in Great Britain)[69] on wage payments in certain cases in which work is not performed (such as economic lay-off or sick leave); such payments are likely to be inter-related with other measures in the field of labour law or of social security. Requirements of equality of remuneration may be mandatory (e.g. in Great Britain and some African countries), but the need for comparability of work to bring them into play probably reduces their relevance. Potentially of great importance are provisions which make it possible to place mandatory ceilings on rates of remuneration or on their rate of increase; [70] such provisions constitute the most striking example of the limits to giving employees the advantage of the "most favourable" law.

The other main subject covered by mandatory provisions regarding remuneration is that of the protection of wages. The provisions in question range from such matters as the form and periodicity of wage payments to the regulation of advances on, deductions from, and attachment and assignment of wages. They often include the requirement that remuneration be paid within the country, in its legal tender.

As indicated, the various mandatory provisions are those obtaining at the place of work; they override what the parties may have agreed in conformity with the law applicable to the employment relation. The question of possible minima can also arise in the converse situation: where the wage agreed in a contract is sufficient under the law of the place of work, but below the minimum required by the law applicable to the contract, is that minimum binding? The question was considered by the Supreme Court of the Netherlands in a decision of 30 May 1980.[71] In a sense, the case was merely one of interpretation of the relevant statute, which made residence in the Netherlands a condition of its applicability. But the judgement provides a wider rationale for not making minimum wage legislation applicable to work abroad by pointing out that such legislation is intimately linked both to the economic situation and to the wage and price levels of the legislating country.

It is not unusual for employees working in a foreign country to arrange to receive part of their remuneration at their home; this arrangement may be due to such factors as continuing financial commitments there, or potential difficulties in repatriating earnings received at the place of work. How can such an arrangement be reconciled with mandatory provisions on the place and manner of wage payments, or even on wage rates? The fact that there is a problem in some countries under legislation governing labour matters or exchange control is reflected in express provisions to meet it in legislation on investment,[72] on joint ventures [73] and on the employment of foreign technicians.[74] However, information on recent examples [75] to show how the matter is handled in the absence of such provisions is not readily available.

Sometimes, for the determination of entitlements to such benefits as termination indemnities, it is necessary to decide what constitutes "remuneration". In an international employment relation, by reference to what law is such a determination made? The problem is one of classification, but not one on which rules of private international law depend; normally, therefore, the determination would be left to the law governing the issue to be decided – that applicable to the employment relation or, as appropriate, the mandatory law of the place of work. A recent decision of the Court of Appeal of Brussels [76] is not very revealing on the subject, in that it found Belgian law to govern the employment relation, while that law was also that of the forum (which had mandatory legislation). On the other hand, the substance of the decision is of some interest; although it treated an expatriation allowance as remuneration, it held that cost-of-living indemnities were merely designed to maintain purchasing power in different countries and did not increase the remuneration itself.

Hours of work

Many States prescribe the maximum hours which may be worked normally, place limits on the amount of overtime, lay down minimum pay supplements for overtime, and specify the frequency and duration of periods of rest. Such provisions are usually mandatory in relation to all work performed in the country. States that have ratified one or other of the ILO Conventions on the subject would indeed seem to be bound to apply their standards to all work in the branches of the economy covered by them.

There is generally no objection to improving in this respect on the mandatory legislation at the place of work. The practical difficulty of doing so by application of the law governing the individual employment relation is that hours of work need to be set collectively rather than individually. Reference was made in Chapter II, section C, to a decision of the Yugoslav Constitutional Court of 12 July 1977 [77] contemplating the applicability of Yugoslav limits on weekly hours of work to workers employed by a Yugoslav engineering undertaking abroad; the Court did so by reference to an express constitutional text creating obligations for the undertaking in relation to all its employees abroad. Collective agreements are another possible means of achieving the collective application abroad of agreed standards on hours of work by employers bound by them; in a case which came before the Finnish Labour Court in 1979 and 1980 [78] (and which will be further considered in Chapter IV), the facts were that the Building Industry Federation and the Building Workers' Federation had agreed that Finnish labour law and the collective agreement should be applied on construction sites abroad, but that their requirements regarding hours of work had not been respected on building sites in Saudi Arabia. It has been suggested by some writers that even the law governing the individual employment relation might be relied upon where the protection given workers by the law of the place of work is inadequate. [79] This approach was followed in a decision of the National Labour Court of Israel in 1982; it considered the provisions of the Hours of Work and Rest Act, 1951, regarding overtime pay and remuneration for work during weekly rest to be applicable to work offshore outside Israel under an individual employment relation that had been found, by reference to the implied intention of the parties, to be governed by Israeli law.[80] Elsewhere, however, legislation concerning hours of work seems to be regarded as limited in its effects to the territory of the legislating State – a view which may have some relation to the normal means of its enforcement.[81] In an admittedly old decision, the Supreme Court of the United States held that the overtime provisions of the Eight-Hour Law did not apply to work done by United States employees for United States employers on construction projects in Iraq and Iran.[82]

Special problems arise as regards certain types of international transport, particularly international road transport. If the countries through which the vehicle passes place different limits on working or driving hours, which applies? The European Agreement concerning the work of crews of vehicles engaged in international road transport (AETR) provides for the applicability of the law of the country in which the driver ordinarily carries out his work, subject to the application of the provisions of the Agreement where their requirements are more stringent. ILO Conventions on hours of work and rest periods in road transport do not deal with the question. In the absence of international agreement, it is likely that the requirements of the law of origin of the vehicle (which would normally be that of the employment relation) and of that of the country through which the vehicle passes both have to be satisfied. In other words, the stricter rule applies in each case. At the same time, the question has arisen whether, for the enforcement of the limits on hours of work and of driving set by law, time spent working or driving in another country must be taken into account. In 1967 that question was answered affirmatively by the highest judicial instance of the Canton of Berne, Switzerland.[83] In 1974 the House of Lords in England came to the same conclusion;[84] it emphasised that any other view would run counter to the aim of preventing the risks due to fatigue.

Holidays with pay

A number of countries make their legal provisions regarding holidays with pay mandatory in respect of all work performed in their territory; this is so, for instance, in Argentina, Belgium, France and a number of French-speaking African countries. The EEC draft regulation on conflict of laws in employment relations would make the minimum holiday of the place of work mandatory. On the other hand, there are countries (including at present some member States of the European Communities such as the Federal Republic of Germany, Italy[85] and the United Kingdom) which leave the matter to be governed by the law applicable to the employment relation.

At the same time, as long as such minimum requirements as there may be at the place of work have been respected even countries regarding the minima as mandatory are prepared to apply the law governing the employment relation. Thus the Court of Appeal of Paris, in a decision of 4 July

1975,[86] accepted that the law of the place of work was less favourable than the (French) law governing the employment relation, and applied the latter. Similarly the Labour Court of Appeal of Brussels, by decision of 11 April 1978,[87] applied Belgian law regarding holiday pay after having found that a contract partially implemented in the Federal Republic of Germany was governed by that law. It may thus be that holidays with pay are one of the areas of labour law in which it is possible for the employee to obtain the benefit of the "most favourable" law, at any rate in certain countries. Such an approach is facilitated by the fact that as regards the two aspects of the subject most likely to be litigious (the length of the holiday and the amount of pay) comparisons between different legal systems are easy.

Occupational safety and health

Requirements regarding occupational safety and health are laid on the employer, and in many countries on the worker, at the place of work. There would seem to be no doubt that the law of the place of work is thus mandatory. It is so described in the draft EEC regulation on conflicts of laws in employment relations. Moreover it is difficult to see how in this respect a law other than that of the place of work could be made applicable through an individual contract of employment.

Nevertheless, there are problems. First, and most important, there is that of (particularly but not exclusively foreign) companies using processes or substances in respect of which the legislation of the place of work does not provide adequate protection. It is of interest that the ILO Tripartite Declaration on Multinational Enterprises, in paragraph 37, addresses itself to this problem at some length: in maintaining standards of safety and health, relevant experience in the enterprise as a whole, including knowledge of special hazards, should be borne in mind; the enterprise should make available to the representatives of the workers in the enterprise, and upon request to the competent authorities and the workers' and employers' organisations, information on safety and health standards relevant to their local operations which they observe in other countries; in particular, they should make known to those concerned any special hazards and related protective measures associated with new products and processes. The Declaration is not legally binding. But there are legal means of achieving the protection aimed at. Where foreign technicians work with the processes and substances, it is possible, through collective agreements and even standardised individual contracts of employment in their country of origin, to achieve the application of protective measures which would have been required in that country. Local workers at the place of work, although probably debarred from making foreign law as such applicable to their employment, can have the substance of the relevant provisions of a foreign law embodied in a collective agreement. In the case of foreign workers, compliance with what has been agreed could be enforced only through the courts;[88] for local workers, labour inspectors might be competent.

Secondly there is the problem of movable workplaces, in particular of ships. On the one hand, many ships carry equipment (such as cranes and ladders) which is used by workers in the ports of different countries. It is not feasible to bring the equipment under a different local law in each case. For this reason, the ILO has sought for over 50 years to achieve some standardisation of laws in this field. In the most recent instrument on the subject – the Occupational Safety and Health (Dock Workers) Convention, 1979 – provision is moreover made for the mutual recognition of arrangements for the testing and certification of gear and equipment. On the other hand, there is the question of the right of the State in which a port is located to concern itself with the conditions of the crew on board a foreign ship normally subject to the law of the flag. Traditionally, such a State has refrained from intervening, although it no doubt had residual authority to do so. A recent ILO Convention, the Merchant Shipping (Minimum Standards) Convention, 1976, expressly provides for the possibility of intervention in certain cases, even as regards ships flying the flags of countries not parties to the Convention. The measures envisaged are to be taken not on the basis of the local law as such but by reference to the international labour standards referred to in the Convention; [89] however, those standards are presumably applied through the local law. A number of Western European countries have, by further informal agreement among themselves, established detailed guidelines for the action to be taken.

Protection of particular categories of workers

Virtually every country has legal provisions for the protection of particular categories of workers, although the range and substance of such provisions varies greatly. For example, there may be prohibitions of assignments of young workers or women to certain tasks or shifts; there may be special entitlements, such as those to maternity leave; special obligations may be laid on the employer, for instance as regards the employment of handicapped or of the otherwise underprivileged persons.

With respect to prohibitions of assignment, what has been said above, in section A, regarding the minimum age for admission to employment, appears to hold good: the law of the place of work is mandatorily applicable. However, where the employment relation is governed by another law which has more stringent requirements than that of the place of work, it is reasonable to expect those requirements to be respected.

The situation would not appear to be markedly different as regards special entitlements such as those related to maternity. In many countries the relevant provisions of the place of work are mandatory. As regards duration of maternity leave and other entitlements at the employer's expense, there is nothing to prevent the application of provisions of a different law governing the employment relation which are more favourable for the employee. However, in so far as maternity benefits are payable from public funds, only the requirements of the law of the country of the institution liable to disburse them will be met.

Special obligations regarding the employment of handicapped persons or of otherwise underprivileged sections of the population are in a somewhat different category. Although they are normally incumbent on all employers active in the territory of the State imposing them, the facts underlying a recent decision of the Supreme Court of the United States [90] suggest that commercial treaties may not infrequently exempt branches of foreign undertakings (but not locally incorporated subsidiaries). There is also a tendency to protect only persons who are nationals of the legislating country or domiciled within it. Moreover, these obligations are so intimately related to demographic and other specific concerns of the country imposing them that their applicability elsewhere is open to question. However, if a handicapped employee, for example, is sent abroad temporarily, he does not thereby lose claims to special treatment under the law governing the employment relation.

Contractual clauses prohibiting competition or disclosure

In certain occupations it is common for the employer to require that the employee, on leaving his employment, should not work for a competitor or otherwise participate in competitive activities, and should not divulge "trade secrets". However, in a number of countries the legislation or the case law reflects an attempt to limit this interference with the employee's right to choose his employment freely. Temporal or spatial limitations are commonly set on the prohibitions regarding competition, or financial compensation is required as a counterpart for the restrictions accepted by the employee; [91] the way in which this is done varies greatly.

In a few countries, provisions on the subject are included in legislation which is mandatorily applicable to all work performed in their territory. This is the case, for instance, in a number of French-speaking African countries. More generally the view appears to be taken that the subject is most appropriately regulated by the law governing the employment relation.[92] At the same time, some writers consider that this is an area in which the public policy of the State of the forum may be relied on to prevent the enforcement of contractual clauses which restrict the right to work too severely; [93] others take the view that this should be done only with the greatest circumspection, given the need to strike a balance between the interests of employer and employee.[94]

Recent case law comes mainly from the United States, and relates to conflicts between the law of different states of the Union. It is not always easy to interpret. There are cases in which the courts have simply applied the law chosen by the parties.[95] Others have applied the law of the place where the work was to be carried out, apparently as governing the employment relation.[96] There are cases in which neither the law chosen by the parties nor the anti-competition covenant are applied, and where that decision is justified by specific reference to the public policy of the state of the forum.[97] In other cases the courts have applied the law of the forum rather than that chosen by the parties, but not exclusively by reference to public policy.[98] By and large the decisions seem to bear out the doctrinal views summarised above.

Some national legislation on the subject expressly adapts the usual requirements for international employment relations. Thus the compensation normally payable under the Commercial Code of the Federal Republic of Germany is not required as regards contracts of employment for work outside Europe.[99] Moreover, it appears that special problems which could arise in international groups of companies are taken into account in practice in the wording of non-competition clauses.[100] Group-wide clauses do not appear to have as yet been tested in court.

Equality of treatment

One final issue needs some discussion. It has been suggested by some writers that international obligations requiring equality of treatment for migrant workers at the place of work are tantamount to making the law of the place of work applicable to the employment relation.[101] Leaving aside the fact, mentioned in Chapter II, that the employment relations of the great majority of migrant workers are in any case subject to that law, is it true that the international obligations in question may negate the choice or applicability of a different law as regards terms and conditions of employment?

A great deal may depend on the terms of the relevant obligation. Some instruments regarding migrant workers, including international labour Conventions on the subject, provide for treatment "at least" as favourable as that given to nationals at the place of work; while they should thus give the worker the protection of a range of local legal provisions going beyond those otherwise regarded as mandatory, there is nothing to prevent the application of provisions of a foreign law which are at least comparable. However, interest in the issue comes primarily from within the European Communities, where EEC Regulation No. 1612/68 on the free movement of workers in the Community, of 15 October 1968,[102] provides that migrants coming from one State Member of the Communities may not be treated differently from nationals in others. Does language like that, particularly when linked to the aim of free movement, mean that the law of the place of work may not be varied to the detriment of either employer or worker, thus effectively preventing the application of any other law?

Case law at the present time is not conclusive. Decisions of the European Court of Justice have given workers the benefit of legal provisions at the place of work in cases in which the applicability of such provisions would otherwise have been doubtful. Thus in 1969 it applied to an Italian worker a provision of the law of the Federal Republic of Germany safe-guarding rights arising out of employment during military service.[103] In 1972 it ruled that the protection from dismissal given to workers suffering from the consequences of an employment injury was applicable to migrants.[104] On the other hand, in a decision of 1974 regarding the application of the law of the Federal Republic concerning the payment of a special allowance for work away from home it was recognised that in regard to such workers' entitlements there might be objective differences between nationals and migrants.[105] However, there do not appear to have been any decisions in which the principle of non-discrimination has been relied upon to exclude the applicability of a foreign law more favourable to the worker than that obtaining at the place of work.

C. TERMINATION OF THE EMPLOYMENT RELATION

In international as in internal employment relations, termination of employment is the largest single cause of litigation. It may accordingly be desirable to consider in more detail the question of the law applicable to different aspects of such termination (grounds, procedure, financial consequences). This is also the field in which most account appears to be taken of the existence of multinational groups of companies, and there accordingly is some material to show the manner in which the normal rules are affected by the existence of such groups.

Grounds for termination

The law of a substantial number of countries places limits on the discretionary power of the employer to bring employment to an end, by requiring justification for such action. However, the extent to which and the manner in which it does so varies greatly; [106] the question of the law applicable to the issue is accordingly an important one.

Many of the States having general labour legislation that is expressly or by implication made applicable to all work within the country include therein provisions regarding dismissal without legitimate reason; this is true, for instance, of the labour codes of a number of French-speaking African countries, and of Angola, Iraq, Mexico, Panama and the United Arab Emirates. In some other countries, such as Argentina and Ecuador, reasons for which dismissal is prohibited (such as absence from work for a limited period of sickness or for military service) are specified. In Great Britain provisions on unfair dismissal are also included in protective legislation which applies irrespective of the law applicable to the employment relation; however, the scope of these provisions depends on the fact that the employee protected does not "ordinarily" work outside the country, and accordingly their protection has in some cases been denied to persons working within the country at the time of dismissal,[107] while it has been given to others working at least partially elsewhere at that time.[108]

In some countries case law has given mandatory effect, in relation to work within the country, to national legislation with provisions on the subject. Thus the Supreme Court of the Netherlands, by decision of 8 January 1971, applied a decree that invalidates a dismissal without "urgent reason" unless it has been authorised to the case of a European director of American Express with his base in the Netherlands, on the ground that the country's labour market was affected.[109] Similarly the Swedish Labour Court, in a 1976 decision, considered that provisions of the Employment Protection Act, 1974, requiring reasonable grounds for giving notice of termination, were applicable to a Swede employed by a Swiss company in Sweden, owing to the "strong connection with" the Swedish labour market.[110] The reasoning of these courts seems to imply that national legislation requiring justification for dismissal would not necessarily be applied, as regards work within the country under a contract governed by a different law, if the national labour market were not affected.[111] Of more general effect is Belgian case law: according to decisions of the Court of Cassation of 25 June 1975 [112] and of the Labour Court of Appeals of Brussels of 20 December 1978 [113] article 20 of the Contracts of Employment (Consolidation) Act, requiring good cause for the termination of an employment relation of indefinite duration, is a "law concerning public order and security" overriding the law applicable to the employment relation as regards work in Belgium.

Elsewhere the matter is left to the law governing the employment relation. For instance, in the Federal Republic of Germany the Federal Labour Court by decision of 10 April 1975 applied United States law, which it found to permit discharge without reasons, to the termination of employment of an airline pilot resident in the country and based there for his employment.[114] Holding that such discharge did not conflict with local public policy, the Court noted that the dismissal would in fact have been possible even under the law of the Federal Republic. It should be noted also that, even in countries which do not give internationally mandatory effect to their legislation on termination of employment in general, the prohibition of dismissals on certain grounds (such as maternity or trade union functions) is likely to be mandatory as part of the legislation protecting the categories of persons in question.

A common ground for termination of the employment relation is redundancy. It presupposes that the employer cannot find work for the employee. This has raised the question whether, in a multinational group of companies, it is possible or necessary to look beyond the employment opportunities within the particular unit for which the employee works at the moment when termination is envisaged. There is no suggestion that this is so for the local staff of that unit; the issue arises essentially for expatriates. There have been isolated court decisions calling for group-wide employment prospection.[115] Of particular interest, however, is article

L. 122-14-8 of the French Labour Code, adopted in 1973, which provides that "if an employee is placed by the company which engaged him at the disposal of a foreign subsidiary to which he is bound by a contract of employment, and he is later dismissed by that subsidiary, the parent company shall be responsible for his repatriation and for obtaining new employment for him that is compatible with the importance of his former duties within the parent company. If the parent company intends, notwithstanding, to dismiss the employee, the provisions of [the Labour Code regarding termination of contracts of employment concluded for an unspecified period] shall apply." The provision applies only to French companies having a dominant position in relation to the foreign subsidiary concerned; at the same time, it appears to apply irrespective of the law applicable either to the original employment relation with the parent company or to that with the subsidiary.[116]

Employment by different members of a multinational group of companies has been relevant, in a different manner, to the justification of termination of employment in Brazil. For the now relatively few workers covered by the relevant provisions, security of employment is attained through relatively lengthy service with the same employer. This raises the question of the relevance, for the calculation of length of service, of employment abroad by members of the same group. As early as 1965, the full bench of the Supreme Labour Court answered in the affirmative.[117]

Procedures of authorisation or consultation

Under the law of a few countries, the authorisation of a public authority or body must be obtained prior to individual dismissals. In a larger number such authorisation is required either for collective dismissals or for the individual dismissal of particular categories of employees enjoying special protection. There are also countries in which some body representative of workers must be consulted and may have to give its agreement. In respect of what international employment relations do these requirements operate?

A public authority or body can act only in the country in which it was established. This does not necessarily mean that it has competence in relation to work performed within the country under an employment contract governed by foreign law. However, such indices as exist suggest that its powers usually extend to international employment relations in these cases. For instance, the decision of the Netherlands Supreme Court referred to above means that all dismissals liable to affect the national labour market are subject to authorisation by employment offices. In another country having authorisation procedures for individual dismissals in general, Iraq, the relevant provisions are contained in legislation mandatory for all workers in the country. The authorisation requirement for the dismissal of particular categories of employees is often contained in the legislation regarding them, which is itself considered mandatory (see above, section B, as regards women covered by maternity protection, and handicapped persons, and below, Chapter IV, as regards workers' representatives). Collective dismissals are of such direct community concern that it is usually assumed that the procedures relating to them are mandatory in relation to all employment within the country.[118] Significantly, the draft of an EEC regulation on conflict of laws in employment relations would include legal provisions regarding the authorisation of a public authority, alone among rules governing termination of employment, among the provisions applicable at the place of work which must be complied with in any case.

The fact that the authorisation of a public authority cannot be given for the termination of work abroad, even as regards employment relations governed by the law requiring such authorisation, perhaps requires some qualification. In particular, there is the need to prevent evasion of the law by dismissal during a temporary mission or detachment abroad; it would seem reasonable to require of an employer operating within the country that he should obtain authorisation for the termination of the employment of an employee ordinarily based within the country. Conversely, there is the question of the views of foreign courts or authorities (particularly those of the country the law of which governs the employment relation) concerning the effectiveness of an unauthorised dismissal in a country where authorisation is required. There would seem to be no reason why they should not consider such dismissal invalid, as being contrary to the mandatory law of the place of work. It is, however, possible that by reference to the considerations discussed above in Chapter II, section D, distinctions may be made according to whether authorisation is needed for reasons related to the protection of the worker or of the national economy.

Consultation of some body representative of workers on individual or collective dismissals is part of a wider area of collective labour law which will be considered in the next chapter. However, there is some case law specifically related to termination of employment in the Federal Republic of Germany which is of interest, particularly as coming from a country in which the subject is considered to be generally governed by the law applicable to the employment relation and not mandatorily by the law of the place of work. By a decision of 9 November 1977,[119] the Federal Labour Court held invalid the termination of an employment relation governed by United States law on the ground that it had not been submitted to the works council; it considered that the relevant legislation was applicable to all undertakings within the country and covered all their employees, that it could not be excluded by individual contract or collective agreement, and that it related to the general authority of the works council regarding the composition of the workforce and thus went beyond the situation of the individual. The Court left open the position of a foreign employer exclusively employing foreign workers; it also pointed out that the role of the works council was only advisory and that the operation of the law governing the employment relation was thus not totally inhibited. The converse situation, namely the applicability of the requirement of consultation for the termination of employment relations abroad governed by the law of the Federal Republic, was considered by a regional labour court on 23 May 1977 [120] and by the Federal Labour Court on 21 October 1980.[121] In the first case the Court took the view that even if the relevant legislation were applicable to a foreign branch of an undertaking established in the Federal Republic, the matter did not fall within the competence of the works council of the undertaking within that country. In the second case the Court held the legislative requirement to be applicable only as regards employees abroad having an organisational link with the undertaking's home base, and not as regards those specifically engaged for work in a foreign country.

Periods of notice

Most countries provide for some notice to be given of the termination by either party of employment relations of indefinite duration, or for compensation to be paid in lieu of such notice. However, the length of the period of notice and the methods of calculation vary considerably.

Again, in a number of countries the relevant provisions are contained in legislation expressly made applicable to all work within the country, irrespective of the law governing employment relations. This is so, for instance, in Angola, Argentina, some French-speaking African countries, Ecuador and the United Arab Emirates. As regards Great Britain, the scope of the mandatory legislation is not defined in the same way for the provisions regarding minimum periods of notice as for those regarding unfair dismissal: they do not apply during any period when the employee is engaged in work wholly or mainly outside the country unless he ordinarily works within the country and the work outside is for the same employer; by implication, they appear to apply to all persons working within the country at the time when the termination of their employment is contemplated.

Elsewhere provisions regarding notice are made mandatory at the place of work by case law. Thus in the case which led the Swedish Labour Court in 1976 to affirm the mandatory nature of the relevant provisions of the Employment Protection Act, one of the complaints made was that the contractually agreed notice was shorter than that prescribed by the Act. The decisions of the Belgian Court of Cassation of 1975 and of the Labour Court of Appeal of Brussels of 1978 held article 15 of the Contract of Employment (Consolidation) Act, specifying periods of notice, to be a "law concerning public order and security" applicable in the country even to employment relations governed by a foreign law.

At the same time, there are, again, countries which leave the matter to be governed by the law applicable to the employment relation. In the decision of 10 April 1975 referred to above, the Federal Labour Court of the

Federal Republic of Germany accepted the termination without notice of an employment relation subject to United States law; it considered at length the question whether such a dismissal was unacceptable in terms of the moral standards and purposes of the law of the Federal Republic, and came to the conclusion that the contrast between dismissal with two weeks' notice (the normal minimum under the law of the Federal Republic) and none at all was not so gross as to raise a question of public policy. There have been analogous decisions in Italy; in particular, in a decision of 26 September 1968,[122] the Tribunal of Milan considered it to be evident that the length of notice was not a fundamental principle of the Italian legal system.

The length of the period of notice is frequently dependent on length of service. The question therefore arises, again, whether service abroad, including service for other members of the same multinational group of companies, is taken into account. Belgian case law has both affirmed that no distinction is made under Belgian law according to whether work was performed in Belgium or abroad,[123] and has taken account of service with independent entities in different countries belonging to the same group.[124] The French legislation, referred to above, concerning the obligations of a French parent company to employees transferred to a foreign subsidiary, specifies that if the parent company dismisses the employee instead of finding new employment for him the time spent in the service of the subsidiary shall be taken into account in calculating the period of notice.

Belgian case law regarding the calculation of the period of notice is also of interest for another reason. National legislation fixes a minimum period of notice; for persons earning more than a specified amount it leaves it to the parties, or the courts, to determine the appropriate period, taking account of such elements as the amount of remuneration and the professional qualifications, in relation to possibilities of re-employment. In a series of decisions, the courts have held that in deciding the period of notice appropriate for the termination of an employment relation governed by foreign law, they will not apply the usual internal criteria, although respecting the mandatory minima. In this connection they have contrasted the approaches of certain foreign companies, in which higher salaries went hand-in-hand with less security of employment, with those of Belgian companies, seeking attachment of the workforce to the undertaking;[125] they have sought to evaluate the employment possibilities on the specific labour market of multinational enterprises;[126] or they have simply referred to the criteria used in the foreign country concerned.[127]

Payments on termination

The special payments made on termination of employment may be of several kinds. There may be compensation for unjustified dismissal; the law applicable thereto is that which determines whether the dismissal was or was not justified. There may be payments in lieu of notice: the law applicable thereto is that which determines the length of notice. There is also likely to be some kind of termination indemnity, in all cases or in certain types of cases such as redundancy. The rules for determining the law applicable to such an indemnity may be independent of those relating to other aspects of termination of employment.

It is particularly difficult in this connection to compare the approaches of different countries, because they may reflect differences in the type of termination indemnity. For instance, one of the considerations which has led Italian courts on several occasions to refuse to give mandatory effect to the Italian long-service grant [128] is that it is regarded as a delayed part of wages; the courts have been prepared to assume that the corresponding element is included in the ordinary annual wage, unless the wage paid under a contract subject to foreign law violates Italian minimum requirements. The relationship to social security entitlements may also play a role in some countries.

That being said, there are again several countries (for instance Angola, Argentina, some French-speaking African countries, Ecuador and the United Arab Emirates) in which the relevant provisions are included in legislation that is mandatory irrespective of the law governing the employment relation. The relevant British provisions again define their scope specifically: an employee who on the "relevant date" is outside Great Britain is entitled to redundancy pay only if he ordinarily works in that country under the contract of employment; conversely, an employee who ordinarily works outside the country under the contract of employment is entitled to redundancy pay only if on the relevant date he is in Great Britain in accordance with instructions given by the employer. Case law has turned on the question whether presence in Great Britain has been on the instructions of the employer.[129]

The question also again arises whether service abroad, including service in legally independent members of the same group of companies, should be taken into account in calculating the amount of indemnity, which is often based on years of employment with the same employer. There is some case law affirming that it should.[130] The French legislation concerning the obligations of a French parent company to employees transferred to a foreign subsidiary specifies that if the parent company dismisses the employee instead of finding new employment for him, the time spent in the service of the subsidiary shall be taken into account in calculating severance pay. It has been pointed out that such an approach may, in certain cases, lead to a plurality of benefits;[131] it would seem, however, that in the majority of cases in which the question can arise there has been unbroken employment within the group.[132]

Notes

[1] Any survey of this subject must make repeated references to two pioneering studies. F. Gamillscheg's *Internationales Arbeitsrecht* (Tübingen, 1959) remains, nearly a quarter of a century later, the most complete and erudite work in the field. B. Knapp's "La protection des travailleurs des sociétés membres du groupe" (in *Colloque international sur le droit international privé des groupes de sociétés* (Geneva, 1973)) was an early survey of the labour law issues raised in private international law specifically by the existence of multinational groups of companies. References below to "Gamillscheg" or "Knapp" are made to these studies.

[2] Knapp, p. 157, and Kahn-Freund, in *Colloque international...*, op. cit. supra, at p. 200.

[3] For instance W. Zöllner, ibid., p. 214.

[4] *Dalloz-Sirey*, 1981, "Jurisprudence", p. 479.

[5] A. Lyon-Caen: "Droit du travail et entreprise multinationale", in B. Goldman and P. Francescakis (ed.): *L'entreprise multinationale face au droit* (Paris, 1977), at p. 297.

[6] Gamillscheg, Section 5.

[7] See for example I. Vacarie: *L'employeur* (Paris, 1979), sections Nos. 224, 226 and 231; J. Mestre and M. Buy, in *Dalloz-Sirey*, 1981, pp. 747-753.

[8] See to this effect A. Lyon-Caen: "La mise à disposition internationale de salariés", in *Droit social*, 1981, pp. 747-753.

[9] H. Kronke: *Rechtstatsachen, kollisionsrechtliche Methodenentfaltung und Arbeitnehmerschutz im internationalen Arbeitsrecht* (Tübingen, 1980). See also the examination of different types of transfer and detachment in R. Birk: "Multinational corporations and international labour law", in *International law problems of multinational corporations* (Heidelberg, 1978).

[10] Vacarie, op. cit. in note 7, section No. 160; Lyon-Caen, op. cit. in note 8; Mestre and Buy, loc. cit. in note 7. For an example of a case concerning a multinational group, see *Droit social*, 1969, p. 513.

[11] Case No. 1402/1980.

[12] Birk, op. cit. in note 9. The French Court of Cassation, in a decision of 23 October 1974, seemed to apply the law of the contract to the effects of a transfer of an undertaking; the decision has been criticised on that point (see Vacarie, op. cit. in note 7, at pp. 167-168, and other sources there cited). Application of the law of the employment relation was also favoured by Gamillscheg, at pp. 237-238.

[13] *Official Journal of the European Communities*, L. 61/1977, p. 26.

[14] Ibid, C. 104/1974, and *Droit social*, 1975, pp. 568 ff.

[15] This was a major concern of the Economic and Social Committee in its comments on the draft. *Official Journal of the European Communities*, C. 255/1975.

[16] Taking at random legislation published in the ILO *Legislative Series* in the last four years, some form of consent is required by the Belgian Act of 1978 on contracts of employment (section 43); the Ecuadorean Labour Code (section 34); the French Labour Code (section L. 117-14); the Spanish Workers' Charter (section 7 *(b)*); the Federal Act of 1980 to regulate employment relationships of the United Arab Emirates (section 21), and Uruguayan Decree No. 287 of 1980.

[17] The employer may be required to be of age, to have certain qualifications, etc. See for instance sections L. 117-4 and 117-5 of the French Labour Code.

[18] Prof. I. Szaszy has indicated that other socialist countries also apply a special rule to contracts of employment (*Ann. Inst. droit int.*, 1971); however, this is not always evident from the relevant legislation. Recourse to the law governing the transaction to determine the capacity to conclude it has been suggested, for contracts generally, by some writers on English law; there is no precedent on the subject.

[19] The application of such general rules is provided for in the draft of an EEC regulation on conflict of laws in employment relations within the Community.

[20] This is so, for instance, under the law of Argentina, Egypt, the Federal Republic of Germany, Greece, Italy, Japan, the Republic of Korea, Kuwait, Portugal, Spain and Thailand.

[21] In the United States the law of the place of conclusion would appear to be generally determining.

[22] This would appear to be the case under the general rules regarding capacity of some of the socialist countries of Eastern Europe.

[23] Taking again only the most recent legislation, see for example section 30 of the Egyptian Labour Code of 1981. The requirement, to be found in the law of some countries, that certain terms of the employment relation shall be confirmed in writing is not a condition of form of the contract itself. It is accordingly governed by the law applicable to the employment relation and, as appropriate, by any mandatory requirements of the law of the place of work where it is different.

[24] See for example the Labour Acts of Kenya and Uganda.

[25] See for instance the Belgian Contracts of Employment Act, 1978, the French Labour Code, the Spanish Workers' Charter, 1980, and Portuguese Decree No. 781/76 on contracts of employment of limited duration.

[26] See for example the Labour Code of Ecuador.

[27] See for instance the Spanish Workers' Charter.

[28] Other common requirements of written form relate to seafarers' articles of agreement and to contractual clauses regarding limitations on competition and disclosure of trade secrets. Countries of emigration frequently require that nationals recruited in their territory for work abroad shall have a written contract before departure.

[29] See for example the aforecited legislation of Ecuador and Egypt and the Argentine Consolidated Rules on Contracts of Employment.

[30] See for instance the aforecited legislation of Belgium, France, Spain and Portugal. Conversely, where contracts for longer than a specified period are required to be in written form, a contract which is not in writing may be assumed to be for less than that period.

[31] See for example the Labour Code of Angola.

[32] This is the case, for instance, in Albania, Costa Rica, Czechoslovakia, England, the Federal Republic of Germany, Greece, Guinea, Italy, the Republic of Korea, Kuwait, Poland, Portugal and Spain.

[33] For instance, under the law of Albania, Greece, Italy, Kuwait and Spain.

[34] For example Argentina, the Central African Republic, Madagascar and Thailand.

[35] See G. M. C. Russomano: *Direito internacional privado do trabalho* (Rio de Janeiro, 2nd ed., 1979), at pp. 171-172. As regards non-local employment in a multinational group Knapp argues (at p. 167) for the cumulative application of the law of the place of conclusion, the law of the place of usual performance and the law of the parent company.

[36] For this purpose, Gamillscheg (at p. 216) ascribed the character of public law to the requirement that the contracts of workers recruited in a country for work abroad shall be in writing or approved by a local authority.

[37] This does not necessarily answer the question whether that law will be applied or taken into account in another country seized of the question of the validity of an employment contract inconsistent with it; in the absence of case law, opinion seems to lean towards an affirmative view.

[38] See for instance article 8 of the EEC Convention on the Law Applicable to Contractual Obligations; article 37 of the 1940 Montevideo Convention on International Civil Law; article 1205 of the Argentine Civil Code; article 4 of the Czechoslovak Law of 1963 on International Civil Law.

[39] See Gamillscheg, at pp. 10 and 230.

[40] See in particular M. Simon-Depitre: "La loi du 3 janvier 1972 sur le travail temporaire et le droit international privé", in *Rev. crit.*, 1973, pp. 277 ff.; G. Lyon-Caen: "Les sociétés de travail temporaire en France et dans la CEE", in *Dalloz-Sirey*, 1971, "Chronique", pp. 93-98; A. Lyon-Caen, op. cit. in note 8; G. Schnorr: "Aspekte des internationalen Privatrechts der gewerbsmässigen Arbeitnehmerüberlassung", in *Z. f. Arbeitsrecht*, 1975, pp. 143 ff.

[41] Such a continuing relation was found to exist by the Court of Justice of the European Communities in the case of a French temporary work agency, for social security purposes (Decision of 8 December 1970, Case No. 35/70).

[42] It could do so where the contract is for any reason, such as the common nationality of

the parties, subject to the law of the country of recruitment. The fact that the employment contract is not affected in any case does not exclude the possibility of penal sanctions in that country against the recruiter and, as appropriate, the employer.

[43] Cases No. 110/78 and 111/78, concerning the placement of theatrical performers. See also a decision of 17 December 1981, in Case No. 279/80.

[44] See for example article 10 (e) of the EEC Convention on the Law governing Contractual Obligations.

[45] See for instance section 66 of the Argentine Rules governing Contracts of Employment; section 2103 of the Italian Civil Code as amended by Act No. 300 of 1970; and section 25 of the Labour Code of the Russian Socialist Federal Soviet Republic. In some countries the employer's authority is limited in effect by provisions specifying that the worker's obligation is that of performing the work for which he was engaged.

[46] See Gamillscheg, at p. 238; Knapp, at p. 169.

[47] Decision of 4 July 1973, *Clunet*, 1975, pp. 359-362.

[48] [1981] *Industr. Rel. Law Rep.* 457-466.

[49] See for example the legislation on private international law of Albania, the Central African Republic, Gabon, Greece, Madagascar and Spain. This is also the position of the highest court in France.

[50] In a few countries (e.g. Hungary and Portugal) legislation makes applicable whichever of these two is more favourable to recovery by the victim. In drafting the Austrian legislation of 1978 that possibility was rejected on the ground that it was often difficult to decide what was most favourable. The Swiss Bill expressly opts for the former, unless injury or damage in another country was foreseeable.

[51] For foreign torts this is the law, for instance, in Egypt, England, Hungary, the Republic of Korea, Kuwait and Thailand. In the Federal Republic of Germany the law of the forum governs liability between nationals. In France and the Netherlands lower courts have sometimes had recourse to the law of the State of the forum by reference to its "public policy". See also decisions of the supreme courts of Nigeria and of Somalia analysed in *Clunet*, 1975, pp. 120 ff. The Swiss Bill would permit the parties to opt for the law of the forum after the occurrence of the injury or damage.

[52] These were, roughly, the facts of a leading Scottish case on the subject: *M'Elroy* v. *M'Alister* 1949 S.C. 110. The situation recurs frequently, particularly across the borders of the different states within the United States, although case law there largely relates to the applicability of workmen's compensation legislation. An analogous problem is that of injury on ships in foreign territorial waters, which was discussed in Chapter II, section C. Also, on cases regarding injuries suffered by Soviet specialists on mission under technical co-operation agreements between socialist countries, see M. M. Bogouslavski in *Clunet*, 1967, pp. 726-732, and *Cours Acad. droit int.*, 1981, I, pp. 401-402. It should be noted that we are not concerned with penal liability, which applies locally only.

[53] For a critical examination of these see O. Kahn-Freund: "Delictual liability and the conflict of laws", in *Cours Acad. droit int.*, 1968, II, pp. 1-166.

[54] See for example J. Foyer: "L'avant-projet de convention CEE sur la loi applicable aux obligations contractuelles et non contractuelles", in *Clunet*, 1976, pp. 555 ff.

[55] For a detailed analysis of the cases see Y. Loussouarn: "La convention de La Haye sur la loi applicable en matière d'accidents de la circulation routière", in *Clunet*, 1969, pp. 5-21. See also on the 1973 Hague Convention on the Law Applicable to Producer Liability, Y. Loussouarn in *Clunet*, 1974, pp. 32 ff.

[56] See Kahn-Freund, op. cit. in note 53, at pp. 106-109.

[57] See for instance the legislation on private international law of Hungary, the Republic of Korea and Thailand.

[58] The traditional English approach is to regard the assessment of damages as a matter of procedure and hence subject to the law of the forum. In the United States some courts have referred to public policy to exclude limitations on recovery under the applicable law.

[59] See E. Groffier: "Le projet de codification du droit international privé québecois", in *Clunet*, 1977, pp. 827 ff.; Kahn-Freund, op. cit. in note 53, at p. 124 (for what he calls "twilight cases"). As regards assessment of damages, this was the approach of the Supreme Court of California in an important 1967 decision (*Reich* v. *Purcell*, 432 P. 2d 727).

[60] This is so in most Western European countries, in French-speaking Africa, in Canada, in Mexico and in Pakistan. There are also general statutory limitations on workers' liability for injury or damage caused in the performance of their work in a number of countries (for instance, Austria, Belgium, Finland, Norway, Sweden, the socialist countries of Eastern Europe), but there is no evidence of their coming into play in international situations.

[61] *A.P.*, Case No. 8 under "IPR Arbeitsrecht".

[62] *Riv. dir. int. priv. proc.*, 1975, p. 737.

[63] See for instance *Busby* v. *Perini Corp.*, 290 A. 2d 210 (Rhode Island, 1972); *Wayne* v. *Olinkneft Inc.*, 293 So 2d 896 (Louisiana, 1974); *Saharceski* v. *Mareure*, 366 N.E. 2d 1245 (Massachusetts, 1977); *Roy* v. *Star Chopper Co. Inc.*, 422 F. Supp. 1010 (federal district court, Rhode Island, 1977). In a 1973 case (*Wilson* v. *Fraser*, 353 F. Supp. 1) a federal district court applied the law of the place where the injury was caused in preference to that under which social insurance compensation had been received; the claim was in fact barred by the choice.

[64] [1971] 1 W.L.R. 1176.

[65] For a technical examination of the problem see L. Collins: "Exemption clauses, employment contracts and the conflict of laws", in *Int. Compar. Law Q.*, 1972, pp. 320 ff.

[66] 1973 S.L.T. 198. The contractual clause provided that remedies were limited to those available under Norwegian law; the contract was governed by Norwegian law.

[67] Provisions on the subject are contained in the consolidated rules on contracts of employment which are mandatorily applicable to work performed in Argentina.

[68] See for example a decision of the Tribunal of Milan of 28 February 1974, in *Riv. dir. int. priv. proc.*, 1976, p. 341.

[69] Under the Employment Protection (Consolidation) Act, 1978.

[70] See for instance section 10 of the Netherlands Wage Determination Act of 1970 and section 3 of the Canadian Anti-Inflation Act of 1975. In some ways akin in result may be an indication, such as that in section 361 of the Swiss *Code des obligations*, that particular provisions remuneration may not be varied to the detriment of either employer or worker.

[71] Due to be published in *Int. Labour Law Rep.*, Vol. 6.

[72] See for example section 20 of the Egyptian law concerning the investment of Arab and foreign capital, as revised in 1977.

[73] See for example section 34 of the Bulgarian Law on Joint Ventures, of 1980.

[74] See for example the Brazilian legislative decree of 1969. The equivalent in local currency of payments made abroad is taken into account for purposes such as inflation adjustment.

[75] Material cited by Gamillscheg, at pp. 308-309, is mostly old.

[76] Decision of 2 March 1980. *J. Trib. Travail*, 1980, pp. 230-231.

[77] *Yugoslav Law*, 1979, No. 3, pp. 67-69.

[78] Due to be published in *Int. Labour Law Rep.*, Vol. 6.

[79] See for instance Gamillscheg, at pp. 274 ff. H. G. Isele: "Auslandsmontage im Arbeitsrecht", in *Festschrift für Hans Ficker* (Frankfurt am Main, 1967), claims that the maximum hours allowed in the Federal Republic of Germany must not be exceeded during temporary assignments abroad.

[80] Case No. MB 2-13.

[81] Enforcement would normally be by inspection services at the place of work, empowered to enforce the local law. Other methods would be used mainly to deal with claims for overtime pay.

[82] *Foley Bros. Inc.* v. *Filardo* (1949) 336 U.S. 281.

[83] Decision of 31 October 1967. *Droit travail et assur. chômage*, Apr. 1968, p. 4.

[84] *Fox* v. *Lawson* [1974] 2 W.L.R. 247.

[85] In a decision of 29 May 1972, the Tribunal of Milan held that while provisions on compensation for unused leave could not be derogated from internally, they were not mandatory in relation to an employment contract governed by English law.

[86] *Rev. crit.*, 1976, pp. 485 ff.

[87] *J. Trib. Travail*, 15 Apr. 1978.

[88] The possibility of trade union action is left out of account in a legal analysis.

[89] ILO: *Record of Proceedings*, International Labour Conference, 62nd (Maritime) Session, Geneva, 1976, p. 193.

[90] *Sumitomo Shoji America* v. *Avagliano*, 15 June 1982. 28 FEP Cases 1753.

[91] The frequent requirement that the clause be in writing has been considered in section A.

[92] See Gamillscheg, pp. 243 ff., and other sources there cited; Knapp, pp. 172-173; Reithmann: *Internationales Vertragsrecht* (Cologne, 3rd ed., 1980), "Arbeitsvertrag".

[93] See G. Müller: "Die rechtliche Behandlung abhängiger fremdbestimmter Arbeit bei Berührung mit Deutschland und Italien", in *Recht der Arbeit* (Munich), May-June 1973.

[94] See Gamillscheg, loc. cit.

[95] See for instance *Associated Spring Corp.* v. *Roy F. Wilson*, 1976, 410 F. Supp. 967.

[96] See for example *Mixing Equipment Inc.* v. *Philadelphia Gear Inc.*, 1970, 312 F. Supp. 1269; 1971, 463 F. 2d 1308.

[97] See for example *Blalock* v. *Perfect Subscription Co.*, 1978, 458 F. Supp. 123; 1979, 599 F. 2d 743.

[98] See for instance *Nasco Inc.* v. *Ginsberg*, 1977, 238 SE 2d 368 (Georgia).

[99] Kronke, op. cit. in note 9. See also section 86 (2) of the Belgian Contracts of Employment Act, 1978, permitting exceptions to the usual rules for salaried employees in undertakings with international business.

[100] ibid.

[101] See for example P. Rodière: "Le projet européen de règlement uniforme des conflits de lois en matière de relations de travail", in *Rev. trim. droit eur.*, 1973, at p. 8; G. Schnorr: *Arbeits- und sozialrechtliche Fragen der europäischen Integration* (Berlin (West), 1974).

[102] *Journal officiel des Communautés européennes*, L. 257/1968.

[103] Decision of 15 October 1969, in Case 15/69 *(Ugliola)*.

[104] Decision of 13 December 1972, in Case 44/72 *(Marsmann)*.

[105] Decision of 12 February 1974, in Case 152/73 *(Sotgiu)*.

[106] For a full recent analysis of legislative provisions on the subject see ILO: *Termination of employment at the initiative of the employer*, Report VIII (1), International Labour Conference, 67th Session, Geneva, 1981.

[107] *Maulik* v. *Air India* [1974] I.C.R. 528; *Ahmed* v. *Janata Bank* [1981] *Industr. Rel. Law Rep.* 457-466.

[108] *Wilson* v. *Maynard Shipbuilding* [1978] 2 W.L.R. 466; *Todd* v. *British Midland Airways* [1978] I.C.R. 959.

[109] *American Express* v. *MacKay*, N.3., 1971, No. 129. It should be noted that it was only in a second decision, two years later, that the Court held the employment relation to have been, in any case, governed by the law of the Netherlands. By decision of 21 December 1982 the District Court of Haarlem applied the decree to the dismissal of a Chilean worker employed on the continental shelf of the Netherlands (Case No. 1402/1980).

[110] *Int. Labour Law Rep.*, Vol. 3, Swe 4. A provision of the contract of employment giving sole jurisdiction to the Swiss courts was disregarded by the Swedish court on the ground that the employee's protection under the Swedish Act was not sufficiently safeguarded thereby. The question of the law governing the contract was not considered.

[111] Kronke, op. cit. in note 9, cites a decision of the District Court of Amsterdam of 13 December 1977 to the effect that civil law rules on security of employment were not mandatorily applicable.

[112] *Pasicrisie belge*, 1976, I, 1038.

[113] *J. Trib. Travail*, 1980, pp. 12-14.

[114] *Int. Labour Law Rep.*, Vol. 2, F.R. Ger. 7.

[115] See for instance a decision of the Court of Appeal of Dakar of 29 April 1969. *Travail et prof. d'outre-mer*, 1971, pp. 6655.

[116] For a discussion of the various aspects of the provision, see G. Lyon-Caen: "Observations sur le licenciement dans les groupes internationaux de sociétés", in *Rev. crit.*, 1974, pp. 439 ff., and the commentary of J. Mestre and M. Buy on two decisions of the Court of

Appeal of Aix-en-Provence in *Dalloz-Sirey*, 1981, "Jurisprudence", pp. 303-308.

[117] See H. Valladão: *Direito internacional privado*, Vol. III (Rio de Janeiro, 1978), at p. 104.

[118] See for example Gamillscheg, at pp. 345-346. The French Court of Cassation on 7 December 1978 (*J.C.P.*, 1979, IV, No. 55) held the requirement of authorisation in case of dismissal for economic reasons to be applicable to a foreign employer.

[119] *A.P.*, Case No. 13 under "IPR Arbeitsrecht".

[120] *IPRspr.*, 1977, No. 44.

[121] *A.P.*, Case No. 17 under "IPR Arbeitsrecht".

[122] *Riv. dir. int.*, 1970, p. 334.

[123] See for example a decision of the Labour Court of Appeal of Brussels of 20 December 1978, in *J. Trib. Travail*, 1980, at p. 13.

[124] See for instance a decision of the Labour Court of Brussels of 28 March 1977, in *J. Trib. Travail*, 1978, p. 337.

[125] See for example decisions of the Labour Court of Nivelles of 1 March 1972, in *J. Trib. Travail*, 1972, p. 88, and of the Labour Court of Appeal of Brussels of 30 June 1972, ibid., p. 246.

[126] See for instance a decision of the Labour Court of Appeal of Brussels of 7 June 1974, in *J. Trib. Travail*, 1975, p. 59.

[127] See for example the decision cited in note 122.

[128] *Indennità de anzianità*. See for instance decisions of the Tribunal of Milan of 26 September 1968 (cited in note 121); 29 May 1972 (*Riv. dir. int. priv. proc.*, 1973, p. 137); and 28 February 1974, ibid., 1976, p. 341; and of the Court of Appeal of Milan, 20 May 1975, ibid., p. 367.

[129] *Roux International Ltd.* v. *Licuidi* [1975] I.C.R. 424; *Costain Civil Engineering Ltd.* v. *Draycott* [1977] I.C.R. 335.

[130] For instance, a decision of the Argentine National Labour Appeal Court of 20 July 1951, cited by E. L. Fermé in A. Vasquez Vialard (ed.): *Tratado de derecho del trabajo*, Vol. II (Buenos Aires, 1982), at p. 897; and a decision of the Court of Appeal of Abidjan, Ivory Coast, of 28 March 1969 (*Travail et prof. d'outre-mer*, 1971, pp. 6973-6974).

[131] Knapp, at p. 175; Lyon-Caen, op. cit. in note 116.

[132] For instance, the Court of Appeal of Abidjan noted, in the above-cited decision, that the employee had worked for the members of the same group without interruption and without being dismissed. However, the French legislative provision requires, as a prerequisite for the obligation of the parent company, that there shall be "dismissal" by the subsidiary.

LABOUR-MANAGEMENT RELATIONS IN PRIVATE INTERNATIONAL LAW

The parties to an individual employment relationship are usually also affected by rules concerning collective labour-management relations. In the present chapter, the question is examined whether those rules are part of the law applicable to the individual relationship, or whether their applicability is determined by distinct methods of choice.

A. EMPLOYERS' AND WORKERS' ORGANISATIONS

In most countries employers' and workers' organisations, particularly the latter, play an essential part in labour-management relations. The overwhelming majority of them restrict their activities to the country in which they are established. For these, the main issues in the framework of the present study are, on the one hand, the guarantee of freedom of association and the right to organise in relation to foreign undertakings, and, on the other, the relevance of foreign elements in the determination of representativity for purposes of recognition. Where organisations seek to extend their activities beyond frontiers, questions also arise regarding the law applicable to such matters as their capacity to act.

Freedom of association and the right to organise

Some multinational and other firms prefer to have a workforce that is not unionised. The ILO Tripartite Declaration of Principles concerning Multinational Enterprises and Social Policy expressly calls on host countries not to include, in special incentives to attract foreign investment, any limitation of the workers' freedom of association or the right to organise and bargain collectively (paragraph 45). If there are no such special limitations, which system of law can be relied upon in the matter?

It would appear that whatever guarantees [1] on the subject may exist in a country should be operative in relation to any employer active there, irrespective of whether the undertaking is a foreign one. This is the clear assumption of the two key ILO Conventions – the Freedom of Association and Protection of the Right to Organise Convention, 1948, and the Right to Organise and Collective Bargaining Convention, 1949 – which have been ratified by about two-thirds of the States of the world. Moreover, the terms of the former Convention, establishing the principle of freedom of association for workers "without distinction whatsoever", imply that such freedom will be guaranteed irrespective of the law governing the employment relation of individual workers concerned. There may nevertheless be problems of enforcement of these guarantees in relation to workers with contracts of employment governed by foreign law: for instance, the most adequate protection against acts of anti-union discrimination is the prohibition of dismissal on the ground of union membership or legitimate union activities; where termination of employment is, as a rule, left to be governed by the law applicable to the employment relation, it would be necessary either to have a special rule on this point or to have recourse to "public policy". If, as is frequently the case, the principle of freedom of association is inscribed in the national Constitution, this fact may provide an appropriate basis for protection.[2]

Where the guarantees at the place of work are inadequate, the question arises whether they can be supplemented by the law governing an individual employment relation, or by that of the home State of the undertaking. The law governing an individual employment relation can protect the employee concerned against acts of anti-union discrimination in so far as the relevant provisions are applicable abroad[3] and do not conflict with mandatory provisions at the place of work. It cannot protect the workforce as a whole, or deal with such matters as the access of union representatives to the premises of the undertaking. The question of the possible application of the law of the home State of the undertaking is in fact that, discussed in Chapter II, section C, of the extra-territorial effect of mandatory legislation.[4] Such application is conceivable but in fact very rarely attempted. And, like the law applicable to the individual employment relation, it finds its limits in the mandatory legislation of the place of work, as in the case of attempts in the last decade to promote freedom of association in South African subsidiaries of European undertakings.

The mandatory legislation of the place of work is also relevant to "negative" freedom of association, i.e. the right not to join a union. Where that law prohibits or qualifies the possibility of concluding union membership agreements, the undertaking cannot rely on the law of its home State, or on that governing individual employment relations, to justify the maintenance of a closed shop. Conversely, it is conceivable that an employee might rely on the law governing his employment to refuse to join a union having a union membership agreement with the employer in accordance with the law of the place of work; in practical terms, this would be more likely to ensure damages for unjustified dismissal in the courts of the home State than the right to work.

Recognition

The primary, though not the sole, purpose of union recognition is to entitle the union to negotiate with the employer or an organisation of employers. The main criterion for recognition is representativity. Evidence of representativity may come from union membership, or from the support given to the union by the workers in the "bargaining unit". What is the account taken, in this connection, of foreign elements?

In a few countries [5] it is a condition of the recognition of unions that at least a specified percentage of their members should be nationals of the country concerned. Within the country, this is an internal problem of the status of aliens, and does not raise issues of private international law. However, in relation to foreign unions which may wish to operate within the jurisdiction of such a country, the provisions in question (as also provisions limiting access to positions of authority within unions) constitute mandatory legislation barring their access.

As regards the relevance of foreign contacts in the determination of a bargaining unit, and the evaluation of the support given to the union seeking recognition, there is case law in the United States. It appears to be settled law that the fact that a particular bargaining unit within the United States includes foreigners does not matter. There has been some hesitation as regards the applicability of the National Labor Relations Act to employers active in the United States but closely connected with a foreign State, but in 1977 the National Labor Relations Board held the Act to be applicable in such circumstances.[6] Persons working outside the country, even though they are United States nationals and employed by a United States undertaking, may not participate in a bargaining unit.[7] Moreover, in two judgements delivered on 18 February 1963,[8] the Supreme Court held that vessels flying a foreign flag and manned by alien crews were not within the purview of the National Labor Relations Act even while they were in United States ports. Some of the considerations advanced in the key case (*McCulloch* v. *Sociedad Nacional de Marineros de Honduras*), which concerned an attempt by the National Maritime Union (NMU) of the United States to represent the Honduran crew of a vessel flying the flag of Honduras but beneficially owned by nationals of the United States and regularly calling at ports in the United States are of interest: in particular the court noted, on the one hand, that the NMU could not represent the crew under the law of Honduras (which required that 90 per cent of the membership of a union had to consist of nationals), and, on the other, that since the crew were members of a Honduran union the claim of the NMU to exclusive bargaining rights would create a conflict.

In matters other than collective bargaining, unions are widely empowered to represent their members. Since there are increasingly numerous arrangements between unions of different countries under which they agree to give each other's members necessary assistance, the question arises whether their authority to act on behalf of members of foreign unions will be recognised. The question was considered by a regional labour court in the Federal Republic of Germany in 1975:[9] by reference to a decision of the national trade union confederation that assistance should be given to members of foreign unions affiliated to the International Confederation of Free Trade Unions (ICFTU), a union of the Federal Republic sought to represent before the labour courts some employees of an undertaking established in the Federal Republic who were nationals of the Netherlands. The court accepted that it should do so, despite the absence of express authorisation from the union concerned in the Netherlands or from the ICFTU.

Capacity to conclude collective agreements

The capacity of an employers' or workers' organisation to perform certain legal acts, such as the conclusion of collective agreements, derives in the first instance from its statutes. Those statutes are governed by the law of the country in which the organisation is established, and are interpreted in that light. If the organisation seeks to act in a country other than that in which it was established, it would seem that its capacity to act is defined and circumscribed by the law of the place at which the legal act is performed. The fact that this principle is somewhat different from that regarding capacity to enter into an individual employment relation (see Chapter III, section A) can no doubt be explained by the fact that labour-management relations are a matter of public policy.

From the point of view of private international law interest in the capacity to conclude collective agreements has centred on two main subjects, namely possible collective agreements covering an entire multinational group of companies and possible collective agreements covering the geographical area of the European Communities. A considerable amount has been written on these subjects.[10] In both cases, organisations are envisaged as acting outside the country of their establishment or on behalf of constituent organisations each remaining in its own country, with effect in a number of countries. In both, the plurality of and divergences in national laws regarding capacity have been assumed to constitute a major obstacle to such action. It is not certain that this is so; where there is a will there is usually a way. However, it would appear that no real attempts are being made to conclude collective agreements of the traditional type with the scope that has just been described. There is accordingly little point in pursuing the legal issues involved further in this survey.

Two developments in actual practice none the less deserve mention. First, there appear to be some national unions whose statutes expressly provide for activities in relation to services and establishments abroad.[11] They probably do so for the purpose of the extension beyond national frontiers of agreements negotiated within them (a question considered in the next section) rather than for negotiation abroad, but the relevant provisions may be open to other uses. Secondly there is one respect in which collective agreements are regularly concluded between parties of different nationalities, including an international federation of trade unions: in many ports, particularly in Europe, agreements regulating the conditions of work of crews on ships flying the flags of various countries are concluded between shipowners of various nationalities and the International Transport Workers' Federation (ITF). In two recent cases, which will be considered further in the next section, an action on the basis of such an agreement was brought in the English courts, in one case by the ITF (as a counterclaim) and in the other by the shipowner. In neither was the question of capacity to conclude the agreement considered as such. The cases nevertheless throw some light on the subject. In one the agreement had been concluded in a British port. The requirements of British law regarding capacity to enter into collective agreements are not difficult to meet.[12] The court found as a fact that the ITF was a trade union in the meaning of the Trade Union and Labour Relations Act, 1974, and, called upon to decide whether there was a collective agreement in the sense of that Act, held that it was so since it was "plainly between an employer and a union".[13] In the other case [14] the agreement had been concluded in Spain, and was signed on behalf of the ITF by an official of a Spanish union of which the crew were members. This would appear to have met the requirements of Spanish law regarding capacity to enter into an agreement. However, a problem of representation arose: the form in which the agreement was signed did not conform to ITF instructions. The question of the effect of this on the obligations of the ITF towards the shipowner has yet to be examined.[15]

An entirely different problem is raised by national legislation specifying the level at which collective agreements may be concluded. Thus in one country collective agreements may be concluded only between organisations;[16] while the organisations may decide that certain terms shall apply only to a particular undertaking, the individual employer may not conclude such an agreement under such legislation. This restriction would not appear to mean that he may not arrive at arrangements with representatives of his workforce, but such arrangements would not have the legal status of a collective agreement.

Availability of information

Workers' representatives can perform their negotiating and other functions effectively only if they are adequately informed on the economic position of the undertakings concerned. In multinational groups of companies it has been a major concern of trade unions to find means of obtaining all information which may be relevant; as implied in paragraph 54 of the ILO Tripartite Declaration of Principles on Multinational Enterprises and Social Policy, this may include information regarding the enterprise as a whole.

From the point of view of conflict of laws, the question arises whether it is possible, through the law of a State in which a subsidiary of a group is established, to obtain information from the parent company or other members of the group abroad. This is the issue raised by two draft directives at an advanced stage of consideration in the European Communities, the so-called "Vredeling proposal" on employee communications, and the seventh directive on company law, relating to consolidated accounts and financial statements. At the time of writing, neither text is in final form. However, it is difficult to see how they could prevent the basing of obstacles to their effective implementation on the law of countries outside the Communities, on the lines of the barriers created in some countries to the reach of the anti-trust legislation of the United States. Indeed, an attempt to create such an obstacle has been initiated in the United States, where a Bill to protect "confidential business information" was introduced in both Houses of Congress in 1981.[17]

B. COLLECTIVE AGREEMENTS

Foreign contacts can affect collective agreements in two major ways. On the one hand there is the question of the applicability of national agreements to situations having foreign elements; this covers both applicability to foreign undertakings and foreign workers within the country concerned and the possibility of extending the scope of the agreements to undertakings or workers abroad. On the other hand, there is the question of (possible) "international" agreements in the sense of agreements concluded between parties from different countries. In examining these various questions one must bear in mind the dual nature of a collective agreement, which is both an arrangement between the parties thereto and a means of establishing standards governing the employment of workers who are not parties to it themselves. It also needs to be recalled that in certain areas of collective labour law national practices diverge so much that the differences may be seen as affecting the very nature of the institution: for instance, a British collective agreement "conclusively presumed" not to be enforceable unless the parties expressly specify the contrary may be only the shadow of a contract, whereas a French agreement "extended" to all employers within its scope, and by that fact to all their employees, has been regarded by some authorities as being more akin to a law.

Applicability of national collective agreements within the country of their conclusion

The applicability of collective agreements as arrangements between an employer or an organisation of employers, on the one hand, and unions or other worker representatives on the other is normally limited, irrespective of foreign elements, to the parties to the agreement. At this level, the foreign element is of importance essentially on the employer side; one of the reasons for urging membership of the branches or subsidiaries of foreign companies in local employers' organisations is the desirability of their being included in such arrangements. The applicability of a collective agreement to the terms and conditions of employment of individual workers, again irrespective of foreign elements, varies: it may extend to all those employed by an undertaking party to the agreement, or only to those who are members of a union party to the agreement; in the latter case, irrespective of legal issues, the extent of membership of foreign workers in national unions is likely to affect their coverage, although it is open to the employer to give effect to an agreement through individual contracts even where the agreement is not otherwise binding.

The "extension" of collective agreements exists in many countries; it makes their standards applicable, by decision of a public authority, to employers and employees who are within the geographical and industrial scope of the agreements but would not otherwise be covered by them. Such extension raises particularly clearly the question of the relevance, to the applicability of the provisions of the agreements, of the fact that the employer is a foreign undertaking or that the employment relation of the worker is governed by foreign law; the latter issue arises also in respect of an agreement which has not been extended, where coverage of the employer automatically extends to his employees. The view is widely taken that an extended collective agreement is akin to mandatory legislation: its standards are intended to embrace all employment within their scope. Thus the report on the EEC Convention on the Law Applicable to Contractual Obligations states that such agreements are among the legal rules of the place of work the protection of which cannot be eluded, under the Convention, by the choice of a different law to govern the employment relation.[18]

There would nevertheless seem to be some limits to the application even of extended agreements. Do they necessarily apply to a foreign undertaking which has no branch or subsidiary in the country, but operates there, under contract, for the performance of a specific job? Do they necessarily apply to foreign workers in the country on a temporary assignment? Some authors have drawn attention to difficulties which may arise in that connection, such as a conflict with a collective agreement of the country of origin of a detached worker; it has been suggested that a distinction might be drawn between provisions dealing with collective matters, necessarily applicable at the place of work, and others.[19] In a decision of 4 May 1977[20] the Federal Labour Court of the Federal Republic of Germany held that a collective agreement extended to the entire construction industry, and establishing a system for funding holiday and bad weather pay, was not applicable to Yugoslav workers temporarily in the country under employment contracts, expressly made subject to Yugoslav law, with Yugoslav subcontractors of a main contractor who was a national of the Federal Republic. The Court based itself on the consideration that even an extended collective agreement was a matter of private law and hence subject to the ordinary rules of private international law. It held, more specifically, that public policy considerations did not come into play because the workers had holiday pay under different arrangements, because the continuation of their employment during the season of bad weather was a problem for their country of origin, and because the competitiveness of employers having the nationality of the Federal Republic was not affected, given the need for administrative authorisation of subcontracting abroad. In a note to the case report, Professor E. Lorenz suggests that the decision is, in fact, limited to the temporary presence of foreign employees of a foreign employer without any base in the country (whose contracts would be subject to foreign law even in the absence of express choice, as indicated in Chapter II, section C) and does not constitute a precedent for the evasion of the requirements of the collective agreement, by choice of a foreign law, in employment relations having less strong foreign elements.

Applicability of national collective agreements outside the country of their conclusion

Where an employment relation is governed by the law of a country other than that of the place of work, the question arises whether the governing law includes collective agreements which would be applicable to similar employment in that other country. The draft of an EEC regulation on conflict of laws in employment relations specifies that the applicable law includes collective agreements "in so far as these are binding on the parties". The 1971 resolution of the Institute of International Law on conflicts of laws in the field of labour law provides that the law to be applied is deemed to comprise collective agreements "provided that these are legally applicable". These provisos leave the essential questions unanswered.[21]

There may, first, be a question of the scope allowed to collective agreements by the law under which they are concluded. For instance, since in the United States the courts have repeatedly affirmed that the National Labor Relations Act and the Railway Labor Act apply only within the United States and have held that persons outside cannot be part of a "bargaining unit" thereunder, it would appear that agreements concluded in respect of such a unit cannot normally be effective abroad; a possible exception is the situation of a person included in a bargaining unit while on temporary mission abroad. Similarly, in France the Court of Cassation has stated that collective agreements apply only within France itself,[22] although there do appear to be some agreements which cover certain situations of detachment. Also, the legislation of some countries specifies that collective agreements may be local, regional or national; in a decision of 1982 the National Labour Court of Israel considered that the definition, in the Collective Agreements Act, 1957, of general collective agreements as being "for the whole area of the State" did not provide guidance on the question of the applicability of such agreements to work abroad.[23]

A second question to be considered is the scope specified in the agreements themselves. There has been little systematic study of practice regarding the application of collective agreements to employment abroad. However, some information from France, the Federal Republic of Germany, Italy and Scandinavia shows that there are agreements which cover employment outside the country in which they are concluded, predominantly in transport and in construction, but also for such persons as technicians and bank officers who frequently go abroad in connection with their work. A recent study of the practice of a sample of undertakings established in the Federal Republic of Germany regarding their employees abroad showed that a quarter of the nationals sent abroad were expressly covered by collective agreements concluded in the Federal Republic, another 45 per cent being covered by virtue of their individual contracts.[24] At the same time, the fact that a number of collective agreements make express provision for certain work abroad does not necessarily preclude the application of agreements which do not make such provision, but which also do not expressly limit their scope to the national territory or some part thereof.

The key issue is, of course, the same as that relating to the applicability of collective agreements within the country in which they are concluded; namely, whether they are binding and on whom. There is the problem of British law, under which collective agreements – important as they are, given the number of issues left to be regulated by the parties rather than by legislation – are enforceable only if that is expressly specified (as it usually is not); the only way in which an unenforceable agreement could be taken into account for an employment relation abroad governed by English or Scottish law is through incorporation, express or tacit, in the individual contract of employment. Elsewhere coverage will depend on whether the employer, or both employer and worker, are bound under the law governing the agreement; depending on the terms used and the purpose of such action, the "extension" of the agreement may or may not affect employment outside the country concerned.[25] The random examples available of collective agreements specifically providing for foreign employment show that overwhelmingly they relate to workers detached by an undertaking within the country.[26] But it is difficult, on the basis of such limited information, to answer the questions of private international law which arise in connection with this issue. Given the independent basis for the effectiveness of a collective agreement, is there any necessary connection between its applicability and the law governing an individual employment relation? It has been suggested by one writer that a collective agreement can apply to an employment relation governed by a law other than that under which it was concluded, as long as the relation has a "base" in the country of origin of the agreement.[27] Is the situation then, perhaps, that there is usually a concordance between the law under which a collective agreement is concluded and the "proper law", under the private international law of the country concerned, of the employment relation to which it applies, but not necessarily any coincidence with the law chosen by the parties?

Some of these questions are illustrated by a case which came before the Finnish Labour Court in 1979.[28] The collective agreement for the construction industry expressly provided that Finnish labour law would apply to the temporary employment on construction sites abroad of Finnish workers engaged in Finland by a Finnish employer. The Building Workers' Federation sued on the ground of non-respect of this provision by a particular construction firm. The firm had provided, in contracts concluded with employees sent to Saudi Arabia, that Saudi Arabian law would apply. The Court considered that the choice-of-law clause in the collective agreement was valid for the type of employment it was intended to cover. It further considered that the choice of the law of the place of work in an individual contract of employment would normally be upheld by a Finnish court. However, it applied section 6 of the Collective Agreements Act,[29] to the effect that any part of a contract of employment which is at variance with a collective agreement applicable thereto shall be void and shall be replaced by the corresponding provisions of the collective agreement. In the Court's view, this substitution followed from the validity of the provision of the collective agreement, apparently on the ground that the employer was bound under Finnish law to observe it in contracts concluded by him.

It may be that a court of a different country, and particularly of the place of work, might reason differently.[30] However, as regards employees temporarily sent abroad, the issue is most likely to be resolved in the country of origin. On the other hand, even that country may have to take account of possible conflicts with the law of the place of work. Such conflicts can arise in relation to provisions of a collective agreement, as in relation to those of the law applicable to the employment relation, where the law of the place of work mandatorily determines certain terms and conditions of employment. They can arise as regards certain matters directly pertaining to the collective agreement itself, such as union security clauses or the reservation of certain benefits to union members. In the above-mentioned Finnish case, it was argued by the employer that the collective agreement could not be valid in Saudi Arabia at all, because under the law of that country terms of employment could only be regulated by individual contract and not by collective agreements. From evidence presented to it, the Court found that, while collective bargaining was not allowed and collective agreements could not be relied on, terms derived from foreign collective agreements could be included in individual contracts of employment, and it decided, by reference to the Finnish Collective Agreements Act, that there was an obligation to include them.[31]

There is also the question of a possible conflict between two collective agreements applicable to the same employment. The issue can arise, particularly where it is sufficient, for the binding force of an agreement, for the employer to be bound (e.g. position of an employee detached by a parent company to a subsidiary, but in some relation with both). Writers diverge on the principle to be applied in such cases: some favour application of the agreement with the closest relation to the employment; some that of the place of work; yet others the one most favourable to the employee. There appear to have been no court cases in which these theories were put to the test.[32]

"International" collective agreements

An "international" collective agreement, in the sense of one between parties of different nationalities, raises above all the question of the law governing its conclusion and its application.

One aspect, namely that of capacity to conclude such an agreement, has been considered in section A. A further question, namely that of form, is of less importance in this context than in that of the individual employment relation, because the written form is very widely required for collective agreements and there is thus little problem of national divergences. The essential question is thus that of the law governing the operation of the agreement, including the validity of certain clauses therein.

The simpler form of international collective agreement is that between an undertaking without an establishment in a particular country, but having operations there, and a union belonging to that country. Examples of such agreements exist in transport, for instance. Since every aspect of such an agreement, other than the nationality and registered office of the undertaking, relates to one country, there would seem to be little doubt that the law of that country applies.

No examples of the converse situation, namely that of a union negotiating in a foreign country, on behalf of its members working in or recruited for that country, with an undertaking or an employers' organisation established there, are cited in publications on the subject. Again, since every aspect of such an agreement other than the origin of the union would relate to one country, it would seem that in this case also the law of that one country should apply.

The agreements, already referred to in section A, between the International Transport Workers' Federation and shipowners are more complex in the sense that they may be concluded in a place which is the seat of neither the company nor the union, and will be effective in respect of moving "territory" of perhaps yet another State. In the two cases regarding these agreements which came before the English courts, the question of the law applicable to them was relevant. A court decided the first, concerning an agreement concluded in a British port between the Federation and a Liberian company, by reference to British legislation (which made the agreement unenforceable), without going into the reasons for so doing.[33] In the second, in which the shipowner sued on the basis of the agreement and the Federation sought to have it declared unenforceable by reference to the British legislation, the court applied the principles of private international law regarding contracts; it decided that Spanish law applied to an agreement concluded in Spain with a view to the recruitment of a Spanish crew under Spanish conditions, for service on a ship flying the flag of Malta but having no other connection with that State.[34]

There are as yet no significant examples of overall collective agreements between an international group of companies and unions dealing with their various subsidiaries, or covering a geographical area larger than one country. The three examples generally given of such agreements are all atypical. One is an agreement, concluded in 1967, and covering Chrysler's workers both in Canada and the United States; not only was the undertaking the same, but also the union, and the legislation of the two countries concerned is very similar. A second is an agreement between a Franco-Belgian group, Glaverbel Mecaniver, and the unions active in its various European subsidiaries, for the sole purpose of establishing a central advisory body.[35] It is nevertheless of interest that, in view of the fact that the subsidiary in the Federal Republic of Germany was not wholly owned, and in order to meet legal requirements in that country protecting minority shareholders, in particular, arrangements were made to submit the agreement to the subsidiary for approval. The final example is that of some understandings between organisations at the level of the EEC on hours of work in agriculture;[36] they are in the form of recommendations addressed to national organisations. No guidance on the law applicable to internationally negotiated agreements can be derived from these isolated cases.

C. WORKERS' REPRESENTATIVES IN THE UNDERTAKING

The concept of "workers' representative" varies; this section will cover trade union representatives, elected representatives and workers' appointees on boards of management. At the same time, because it is necessary in private international law to make a sharp distinction between the first two cases and the third, the term "representation" will be used for the former and the term "participation" for the latter; this is not wholly accepted usage.

National legislation regarding workers' representatives shows greater differences than that in respect of any other subject examined so far: in some countries there is no legislation; in some it is limited to provisions regarding the protection of representatives and facilities to be made available to them; in others (e.g. Austria, France, the Federal Republic of Germany, Norway, Sweden, Spain) there are sophisticated institutional arrangements. In these circumstances the effects of foreign contacts are of particular importance. Not surprisingly, most of the information regarding them comes from countries with the most sophisticated systems.

Questions arise as regards the applicability of the law of a particular country to the need to have representatives or participation systems, to the geographical scope of the arrangements and to the protection of representatives. The undertaking is naturally the focus of connecting factors determining the law to be applied. Here the consequences of the fact that an undertaking has establishments in several countries, or that a group is multinational, assume key importance.

The need to have representatives or participation systems

The application of national requirements concerning the establishment of representation or participation systems to undertakings with foreign elements differs according to whether it relates to representation of workers in relation to management, on the one hand, or to participation in management on the other. As regards the former, there are further differences according to the level at which representation is required.

There would seem to be little doubt that, in so far as legal requirements in a country bear on representation in every establishment, these requirements must be met by every establishment within the jurisdiction of that country, irrespective of whether it is a dependent branch or legally autonomous subsidiary of a foreign undertaking. There is judicial authority, as regards this level of representation, only in the Federal Republic of Germany, where the Federal Labour Court affirmed, in a decision of 9 November 1977 [37] that the Works Constitution Act of 1972 was applicable to all establishments in the country. However, the interpretation placed in practice on relevant legislation elsewhere, as reflected inter alia in legal writings, is the same. The only margin of doubt relates to the position of an establishment of a foreign undertaking which employs foreign workers exclusively (or a group of foreign workers employed by a foreign employer on a worksite assimilated to an establishment). This point was expressly left open by the Court. It parallels, in some ways, the position taken by the same Court as regards the applicability of mandatory collective agreements (see above, section B). And it is analogous to the view of the Supreme Court of the United States that the National Labor Relations Act does not apply to foreign crews on ships flying a foreign flag in ports in the United States (see above, section A, and below, section D).

More difficult questions arise if undertakings which have several establishments are required to have a central works council but only some of the establishments of a foreign undertaking are within the geographical scope of the law. This was the problem brought before the full bench of the French *Conseil d'Etat* on 29 June 1973: [38] a company having its principal place of business in Belgium, but several establishments in France, had set up five works committees, but no central works committee. The government departments concerned proceeded on the assumption that this was not required of a company with headquarters abroad. The court, seized by a union, disagreed: the relevant legislation was applicable to any person or body exercising the responsibilities of an employer in France; a foreign undertaking had to set up a central works committee at the place where its main activities as employer within the country were exercised; and such a committee had to be enabled to carry out all the functions given it by the legislation, with the exception only of those incompatible with the fact that company headquarters were abroad. Analogous decisions have been given in the Federal Republic of Germany, not as regards the central works council (regarding which there appears to have been no dispute in practice), but with respect to the finance committee *(Wirtschaftsausschuss)* which must, under the Works Constitution Act, be set up at the level of the undertaking. In decisions of 1 October 1974 and 31 October 1975,[39] the Federal Labour Court affirmed the requirement that such a committee should be set up by foreign undertakings whose principal place of business was abroad in respect of their establishments in the Federal Republic, at least to the extent that those establishments had a certain unity of purpose. The view has moreover been taken by some authors in the Federal Republic that the special provisions in the Works Constitution Act concerning groups of companies *(Konzerne)* can be applied, where the dominant undertaking is abroad, by means of the creation of a "partial" group works council, at least where one of the subsidiaries in the Federal Republic has a certain authority in relation to the others.[40]

These various decisions may not altogether meet the underlying practical problem. The bodies in question (central works committee or council, finance committee, group works council) are intended to give staff representatives access to top management. This is not necessarily ensured by the establishment of such bodies in one country while top management is in another. In this connection, the consideration within the European Communities of the so-called Vredeling proposal on employee communications[41] is of some significance. The draft text prepared by the Commission in 1980 sought, with respect to transnational groups of companies, to give staff representatives access to the dominant undertaking in one country in case information or consultation requirements were not adequately met by a subsidiary in another; it also envisaged the possibility of setting up group-wide bodies representing employees by agreement between the management of the dominant undertaking and the employees' representatives. Amendments adopted by the European Parliament in October 1982 have considerably reduced the possibilities of approaching the management of the dominant undertaking, while leaving it to the undertaking to decide at what level consultation is to take place.

This may be one illustration of the practical limits to the effectiveness of workers' representation in relation to management abroad. Another is the problem of obtaining information, which has been touched upon in section A. At the same time, the extent of the powers available to workers' representatives must not be underestimated. An example is the power given by the law of the Netherlands to a works council to ask the Company Division of the Court of Appeal to investigate the management of the company in which it operates. Writers on the subject have expressed the view that such a provision cannot be used in relation to multinational companies with a foreign base.[42] Yet this was done in 1979 to prevent the transfer of the Amsterdam branch of one such company to Brussels, and in 1981 in an attempt to prevent the closure of the assembly plant in Amsterdam of another.[43] In the first case the Company Division set the transfer decision aside. It held that there had been serious dereliction of the duty to consult, and that this was tantamount to mismanagement. In the second, a district court first decided that the plant had to be kept open pending consideration by the Company Division, in part by reference to the fact that the real decisions were not taken locally and that the powers of co-decision given by the local law thus did not have the intended influence; the Company Division then held that the management was justified in closing the plant. No doubt obstacles could be placed in the way even of such judicial procedures. Nevertheless, these cases are examples of the possibilities inherent in national law regarding workers' representatives in relation to foreign companies.

The problem regarding participation in management is quite different. Such participation, whether on boards of directors or supervisory boards, affects the structure of the company, and it is difficult to see how it can be provided for by any law other than that under which the company is constituted. Accordingly, it appears to be the general view that legislation regarding participation in management cannot be applied in respect of undertakings which have been established and have their principal place of business abroad.[44] This has been expressly recognised in some legislation.[45] At the same time, it raises the possibility of the evasion of national legislation by the establishment of foreign holding companies and the like. One response to this has been to recognise the foreign character of an undertaking or group only where it employs larger numbers of persons abroad than within the country in which the law provides for workers' participation in management.[46] It has also been suggested that if mergers with or take-overs by foreign companies are contemplated, States whose legislation provides for some form of worker participation should give the workers' rights to such participation protection analogous to that given to the rights of shareholders.[47]

Geographical scope of representation and participation systems

The question of the geographical scope of representation and participation systems arises in two main respects: that of the workers on whose behalf the functions of workers' representatives are exercised, and that of the workers and work units entitled to take part in the system, by means of elections or otherwise.

The general approach appears to be to recognise the authority of workers' representatives to represent employees who are temporarily abroad while retaining a base within the country or the undertaking. However, the recognition goes no further. For instance, under section 119 of the British Employment Protection Act, 1975, the provisions of the Act regarding the consultation of trade union representatives on redundancies do not apply if under his contract of employment the employee ordinarily works outside Great Britain. By a decision of 21 October 1980[48] the Federal Labour Court of the Federal Republic of Germany held that while the requirement of consulting the works council on dismissals applied to detached workers with a link to the internal organisation of the undertaking within the country, it did not extend to an employee specifically recruited for employment abroad, however temporarily. At the same time, there is not necessarily unanimity concerning the range of the possible functions of workers' representatives in relation to detached workers. Thus one regional labour court of the Federal Republic held, on 14 February 1979,[49] that although provisions of works agreements applicable within the country could continue to apply to such workers, the powers given to works councils to negotiate works agreements did not extend to establishing conditions exclusively for foreign worksites. Another regional labour court affirmed, on 12 March 1980,[50] that the works council could organise sectional meetings at foreign construction sites as long as the manner of so doing complied with local law.

As regards the inclusion of workers and work units in the selection of individuals for representation and participation systems, such information as there is shows an analogous attitude. Employees who are temporarily detached from, but retain a link with an undertaking within the country also keep their rights to vote and their eligibility. This was affirmed as a matter of principle in relation to the Works Constitution Act, 1972, by the Federal Labour Court of the Federal Republic of Germany in a decision of 25 April 1978,[51] and applied in practice, by a decision of 17 September 1974 of the same Court,[52] to the case of ships' officers detached by a shipping undertaking of the Federal Republic to ships flying a foreign flag. Whole work units abroad may be covered by national legislation as long as the entire unit consists of workers subject to national law. Again, this was affirmed, as a matter of principle, by the above-cited decision of 25 April 1978 in the Federal Republic of Germany. It is apparently the practice of some socialist countries of Eastern Europe.[53] Beyond that national law in the matter apparently does not attempt to go. Thus, in the aforecited decision of 25 April 1978 the Federal Labour Court of the Federal Republic of Germany set aside the election, to a works council in Frankfurt am Main, of an employee permanently working in a branch of the undertaking in Switzerland. Similarly, with respect to the Co-Management Act, 1976, a regional court held on 5 June 1979 [54] that only workers within the Federal Republic could participate in elections for the supervisory board of the dominant undertaking, established there, of a group of undertakings located in the Federal Republic and the Netherlands; it did so both by reference to the proceedings leading up to the adoption of the Act and in the light of the consideration that giving rights to workers abroad and imposing corresponding obligations on their employer would improperly extend legislation giving expression to national socio-political concepts into the area of sovereignty of a foreign legislature. All this means that the foreign subsidiaries of an undertaking, whether separately incorporated or not, are not taken into account in determining the threshold number of workers bringing certain legislative provisions into operation,[55] and that persons regularly employed there can neither vote nor be elected. As regards bodies such as central works councils or committees and group works councils, it has been pointed out that in so far as they are made up of representatives of councils or committees at establishment level, it is presupposed that these lower councils or committees are all constituted in the same manner. Since establishments abroad are in principle subject to the workers' representation system of the country in which they operate, and since the various national systems are hardly ever the same, the need to fulfil this assumption creates a supplementary obstacle to the inclusion of such establishments in the representation system of the country where the undertaking has its head office.

Protection of workers' representatives

In rules for the protection of workers' representatives both individual and collective interests are at issue. The individual representative is protected against dismissal and other acts prejudicial to the rights arising from his employment. He is so protected in order to ensure his independence in the exercise of his collective representative function. In terms of the determination of applicable law, it would seem that the collective interest has primacy. The representative must enjoy the protection of the law in pursuance of which he exercises his functions, whatever may be the law governing his employment. Conversely, the law applicable to his employment cannot help him if his functions are not carried out within the scope of its relevant provisions.

Indeed, in countries having sophisticated institutionalised representation systems, it is usual for the legislation establishing these systems to provide also for the protection of representatives: this is so, for instance, in Austria (Chapter 4 of Part II of the Collective Labour Relations Act); France (articles L. 436-1 and 436-2 of the Labour Code); the Federal Republic of Germany (section 78 of the Works Constitution Act); the Netherlands (section 21 of the Works Council Act); and Spain (section 68 of the Workers' Charter). Elsewhere, the relevant provisions may be contained in legislation which is otherwise mandatory at the place where the undertaking or establishment operates; this is so, for instance, in Great Britain and in some French-speaking African countries. Moreover, in a number of countries, particularly in Latin America, dismissal of workers' representatives requires prior authorisations by a court or labour inspector and is thus necessarily linked to the area in which these public authorities function. The same may be true of the requirement, in certain Eastern European countries, of the consent of some central trade union body for the dismissal of trade union representatives.[56]

D. COLLECTIVE DISPUTES

Peaceful methods of settling collective disputes do not appear to raise major questions of private international law. Where machinery for conciliation or arbitration is established by national legislation, there would seem to be little doubt that its operation is limited to the territory of the country concerned.[57] Furthermore, given public interest in the peaceful settlement of disputes, such machinery must be presumed to be at the disposal of branches of foreign undertakings in the country; in so far as recourse to certain procedures is mandatory, this is likely to be compelling also in relation to such branches. Where machinery for conciliation or arbitration is established by collective agreement or other arrangement between the parties, it will follow the rules regarding the law applicable to collective agreements or works agreements, as the case may be (see sections B and C above). The same would appear to be true of peace obligations contained in or linked to the validity of collective agreements.

A wider range of issues is posed by various forms of industrial action, and in particular by strikes, sympathy strikes and boycotts as well as by certain responses thereto. They have an individual as well as a collective aspect.

The individual aspect consists, on the one hand, in "the right to strike" as an offshoot of the worker's freedom of association for the protection of his occupational interests and, on the other, in the potential effects on his employment of participation in a strike. It appears to be the general view that the legality of strike action can be judged only according to the law of the place where such action is taken (i.e. the law of the place of work), and that a wider right to strike under a different law governing an individual employment relation cannot serve to justify participation in a work stoppage which is not permissible at the place of work.[58] Two judicial decisions appear to confirm that view; however, in both cases the law governing the employment relation was in fact that of the place of work. By a decision of 8 October 1969,[59] the French Court of Cassation affirmed that a French company was justified in terminating the contract of a French worker who had participated, on a worksite in the Virgin Islands, in a strike which was unlawful under local law. In a decision of 6 November 1974 [60] the Tribunal of Genoa held that the restriction of the right to strike of an Italian seafarer under the Liberian law of the flag (which led to his dismissal for refusal to sail) was not contrary to Italian public policy. In this connection, it relied in part on the fact that Italian law also recognised the possibility of restrictions on the right to strike and thus perhaps left open the possibility of a different finding, by reference to public policy, in relation to a total prohibition of strikes. Such a different finding could have importance mainly in relation to the effects of participation in a strike on the employment relation, and there, in any case, views vary. According to some, consequences such as the payment or withholding of wages, dismissal, the payment or withholding of termination indemnities, are necessarily subject to the same law as the legality of the strike; [61] a practical consideration in support of that view is the problem of equal treatment of the employees participating in the strike. Others consider that it is possible for the effects of strike action on the individual employment relation to be governed by the law applicable to that relation, where it is more favourable.[62] In the French case cited above, French law was applied to the question whether the fault involved in the strike action was such as to deprive the worker of indemnities in lieu of notice and holidays; the Court did so on the somewhat spurious ground that the relevant provisions of the law applicable at the place of work had not been cited in evidence before it.

As regards the collective aspect, the first question which arises is that of the reach of national legislation authorising certain types of industrial action and giving unions and their officers corresponding immunities from civil or penal action. In two cases concerning ships flying a foreign flag and manned by foreign crews, which were in United States ports, the Supreme Court of the United States affirmed, in this connection also, that the National Labor Relations Act did not apply to situations that were essentially foreign. In *Benz* v. *Compania Naviera Hidalgo*, decided on 8 April 1957, damages were awarded against officers of United States unions which supported a wildcat strike of the foreign crew of a vessel sailing under the Liberian flag and owned by a Panamanian company.[63] In *Windward Shipping* v. *American Radio Association*, decided in 1974, the Court refused to apply the National Labor Relations Act in a suit to enjoin United States unions from picketing against low wages paid to foreign crews on foreign-owned vessels.[64] A decision in the opposite sense was given in England by the House of Lords on 25 October 1979: [65] it held that the blacking of a ship owned by a Hong Kong company with a Swedish controlling interest, and operated by a Hong Kong crew, was action in pursuance of a "trade dispute" in the meaning of section 29 (1) of the Trade Union and Labour Relations Act, 1974. For this purpose it considered that the International Transport Workers' Federation had to be regarded as "workers" in the meaning of that Act, in spite of the fact that it was an international federation of unions and of the fact that none of the crew were members of an affiliated union; it held that there was a dispute not only between "workers and employers" on conditions of work, but also between "workers and workers" since the crew did not in fact want the Federation to intervene. However, the Employment Act, 1982, has so amended the definition of "trade dispute" as to make the decision irrelevant for the future.

The last-cited decision raises a second issue, namely that of internationally organised boycotts and the related questions of private international law. In his opinion, Lord Diplock referred to the fact that the blacking at issue was part of an international boycott as an argument against enjoining the union – an international federation – not to take industrial action, on the ground that it was beyond the authority of the court to issue an injunction which might be supposed to have effect abroad; he was critical of the fact that in an earlier case,[66] in which the decision had been overruled by the House of Lords for other reasons, an English court had enjoined the blacking of a ship in a Scottish port. Similar questions came before the courts of the Federal Republic of Germany in two cases in which unions set up within the Republic obtained the support of other unions affiliated to the International Transport Workers' Federation in an attempt to compel small shipowners to accede to collective agreements concluded in the Federal Republic. In a decision of 8 August 1973 [67] a regional labour court upheld injunctions issued by a lower court (on the ground that the measures taken went beyond what was reasonably necessary to achieve the ends sought) apparently without considering the implications of the fact that the boycott, although initiated by the unions of the Federal Republic, was at the time being carried out in the United Kingdom and the Netherlands. On the other hand the Federal Labour Court, in a decision of 19 October 1976,[68] did take the foreign element into account: in a case in which the shipowner had signed an agreement to accede to the collective agreement while his ship was being blacked in Denmark, and subsequently challenged the validity of his own signature under duress, it held that boycotts were not inherently unlawful, but that the legality of the action in the particular case had to be further examined, in part in the light of Danish law.

A third issue is that of international sympathy action, i.e. of industrial action in one country in support of strikes in another. As in the case of other forms of industrial action, its legality is determined by the law of the place where the sympathy action is taken. That legality depends, on the one hand, on restrictions which may be put in the country on sympathy action in general, the most usual requirements in that respect being that the strike being supported must itself be lawful and that the sympathy action must have a direct connection with it.[69] The legality also depends both on special rules which may apply to the support of foreign strikes and on the manner in which the general restrictions are applied to foreign situations.

It is rare for national legislation to deal specifically with industrial action relating to foreign disputes. One exception is section 29 (3) of the British Trade Union and Labour Relations Act as amended by the Employment Act, 1982: it provides that "there is a trade dispute, even though it relates to matters occurring outside the United Kingdom, so long as the person or persons whose actions are said to be in contemplation or furtherance of a trade dispute relating to matters outside the United Kingdom are likely to be affected in respect of one or more of the matters specified in subsection (1) of this section by the outcome of that dispute". Similarly, court decisions on support of foreign strikes are isolated and relatively old: the Swedish Labour Court held in 1961 [70] that such support was possible; a much criticised decision of a court of first instance in the Federal Republic of Germany in 1959 [71] held that it was not.

As regards the manner in which general restrictions may be applied to foreign situations, the main issue is whether the legality of the primary strike is decided by reference to the law of the country in which it takes place or by reference to the law of the country in which the sympathy strike takes place. The court of the Federal Republic of Germany in the abovementioned decision assumed the latter, and regarded the impossibility of applying the legal notions of one country to industrial action in another as one reason for not permitting sympathy action at all. Such an approach also has some political implications as regards industrial action in support of workers in countries which severely restrict the right to strike. Moreover, it would be an exception to the general principle of determining the legality of any industrial action by reference to the law of the place where it is taken. Nevertheless, writers are divided on the issue.[72]

What of measures to meet industrial action which may be open to the employer? It would seem that the legality of a lock-out, like that of a strike, must be determined by reference to the law of the country in which such a measure is taken. That law would also have to decide incidental questions such as whether it is permissible to treat different members of the workforce differently, by reference, for instance, to their expatriate status. Another possible measure with international implications, which has been much to the forefront in recent years, is that of bringing workers from a foreign country to act as strike-breakers. Again, it would seem that the admissibility of such action must be judged by reference to the law of the place of the strike; one writer has examined the question whether the law of the country of origin of the workers could play a role and has answered it in the negative.[73] At the same time, the criticism which followed recourse to such a measure by a multinational company in Denmark, in 1976, resulted in the sole modification to be made in 1979 to the 1976 OECD Guidelines for Multinational Enterprises: in language closely akin to that which had, in the meantime, been embodied in paragraph 52 of the ILO Tripartite Declaration of Principles concerning Multinational Enterprises and Social Policy, paragraph 8 of the Guidelines now calls on enterprises not to transfer employees from their component entities in other countries in order to influence bona fide negotiations with workers' representatives unfairly or to hinder the exercise of a right to organise.

Notes

[1] Such guarantees might include not only the protection of workers in the undertaking against dismissal or other acts prejudicial to them by reference to union membership or legitimate union activities, but also such matters as access of union representatives to the premises of the undertaking.

[2] See in this connection, with particular reference to the Federal Republic of Germany, R. Birk: "Internationales Tarifvertragsrecht", in *Festschrift für Günther Beitzke* (Berlin (West), 1979).

[3] It may be recalled, for instance, that the British provisions on dismissal on the ground of union membership or union activities do not apply to an employment relation governed by English or Scottish law if the work performed under it is "ordinarily" outside Great Britain.

[4] On the possible role of collective agreements, see section B.

[5] For instance, Colombia, Panama, the Philippines and Togo. A few others make membership of unions subject to conditions of residence within the country.

[6] Decision of 20 May 1977 concerning the State Bank of India, *Int. Legal Materials*, 1977, p. 853.

[7] *Airline Stewards and Stewardesses Association International* v. *Northwest Airlines Inc.* (1959), 267 F. 2d 170; *Int. Law Rep.*, Vol. 28, pp. 115 ff. The persons concerned were in fact foreign nationals, but the court made it clear that there was no distinction on the ground of nationality. The legislation involved was the Railway Labor Act and not the National Labor Relations Act. A parallel case against Trans-World Airlines (273 F. 2d 69) had an analogous result.

[8] *McCulloch* v. *Sociedad Nacional de Marineros de Honduras*, 372 U.S. 10; *Incres Steamship Co., Ltd.* v. *International Maritime Workers Union*, 372 U.S. 24; *Int. Law Rep.*, Vol. 34, pp. 51-69.

[9] Regional Labour Court of Lower Saxony, 5 November 1975, *IPRspr.*, 1975, No. 31. A 1964 decision of the Federal Labour Court (*A.P.*, Case No. 9 under "IPR Arbeitsrecht") shows that there may be agreements between unions of different countries under which members of one union are automatically members of the other when in the latter's country. Under that decision such membership had the effect of making a collective agreement applicable.

[10] Two examples are G. Lyon-Caen: "Négociation et convention collective au niveau européen", in *Rev. trim. droit eur.*, 1973, pp. 583 ff. and 1974, pp. 1 ff.; and S. Walz: *Multinationale Unternehmen und internationaler Tarifvertrag* (Baden-Baden, 1981).

[11] For instance K. Friedrich: "Probleme der Tarifverträge mit Auslandsberührungen", in *Recht der Arbeit* (Munich), 1980, pp. 109 ff., cites the example of the union of workers in public services, transport and communications of the Federal Republic of Germany.

[12] Under section 28 (1) of the Trade Union and Labour Relations Act, 1974, an organisation is a trade union if it consists of one or more categories of workers and has as a main purpose the regulation of relations between workers in these categories and employers, or if it consists of affiliated unions meeting that description and has as a main purpose the regulation of relations between workers and employers. No further condition has to be met to conclude collective agreements.

[13] *Universe Tankships Inc. of Monrovia* v. *International Transport Workers' Federation*, Queen's Bench Division, 2 April 1980, [1980] *Industr. Rel. Law Rep.*, p. 239. The case was the subject of an appeal, but not on the point considered here. It is nevertheless of interest that, in a different context, the shipowner conceded before the Court of Appeal that the Federation was a union in the meaning of the Trade Union and Labour Relations Act ([1980] *Industr. Rel. Law Rep.* at 367).

[14] *Monterosso Shipping Co. Ltd.* v. *International Transport Workers' Federation*, Court of Appeal, 28 May 1982. *Financial Times* (London), 15 June 1982, "Commercial Law Report".

[15] The only issue examined so far was the preliminary one of the law applicable.

[16] See the definition of capacity to conclude collective agreements in section 4 of the Austrian Collective Labour Relations Act of 1974 (*L.S.*, 1973, Aus. 2).

[17] See D. F. Vagts, in *Amer. J. Int. Law*, 1982, p. 592.

[18] Report on the Convention by M. Giuliano and P. Lagard, *Official Journal of the European Communities*, C. 282/1980.

[19] See for instance G. Lyon-Caen: "La convention collective de travail en droit international privé", in *Clunet*, 1964, pp. 247 ff.

[20] *A.P.*, Case No. 30 under section 1 of the Collective Agreements Act (TVG) *"(Tarifverträge: Bau)"*.

[21] This has not prevented occasional court decisions merely linking the application of a particular system of law and of a collective agreement concluded thereunder. See for instance a decision of the Tribunal of Rome of 26 February 1974 (*Riv. dir. int. priv. proc.*, 1974, p. 622).

[22] See for example a decision of 29 May 1963 (*Clunet*, 1964, p. 301), denying the representative in Italy of a French company an indemnity for non-competition in accordance with the collective agreement for the glass industry. However, the terms of the judgement seem to leave open the possibility of express clauses extending the scope of agreements abroad.

[23] Case No. MB 2-13.

[24] H. Kronke: *Rechstatsachen, kollisionsrechtliche Methodenentfaltung und Arbeitnehmerschutz im internationalen Arbeitsrecht* (Tübingen, 1980).

[25] In a decision of 1982 (Case No. MB 2-13), the National Labour Court of Israel held such an agreement to be applicable to work offshore outside Israel under an employment relation between the subsidiary, incorporated in Israel, of a United States corporation and an Israeli worker.

[26] One example to the contrary is cited by Friedrich, op. cit. in note 11: the agreement between the "Goethe-Institut" of the Federal Republic of Germany and the union of workers in education and science applies to employees abroad who are locally recruited, as long as they are nationals of the Federal Republic. On the other hand, one reason which has been given by Italian unions for the fact that relatively few of the very substantial number of Italian workers employed on projects abroad are covered by Italian collective agreements is that a high proportion of them are specifically recruited for such projects and not linked to any undertaking in Italy.

[27] See Walz, op. cit. in note 10.

[28] Due to be published in *Int. Labour Law Rep.*, Vol. 6.

[29] *L.S.*, 1946, Fin. 2.

[30] In a very old decision of the Austrian Supreme Court, the view was taken that local law was applicable to a foreign collective agreement extended to a subsidiary, within Austria, of a foreign company. See W. Geppert: "Arbeitsverhältnis und arbeitsbezogene Vorschriften im internationalen Privatrecht", in *Das Recht der Arbeit* (Vienna), 1970, at pp. 140-141.

[31] This was the method contemplated in a workers' proposal submitted in 1979 to an ILO meeting of experts on the problem of foreign workers in the construction industry.

[32] But see a decision of the Supreme Court of Buenos Aires of 21 November 1950, in *D° del Trabajo*, 1951, p. 95, holding that a construction worker was subject to the collective agreement of the place of work and not of that of the place where his employment contract had been concluded (which was also his place of normal residence).

[33] Case cited in note 13.

[34] Case cited in note 14.

[35] For a detailed description of this example see J. Rojot: *International collective bargaining* (Deventer, 1978). Some French unions refused to sign the agreement on the ground that it contained no real commitment.

[36] See Lyon-Caen, op. cit. in note 10.

[37] *A.P.*, Case No. 13 under "IPR Arbeitsrecht".

[38] *Rev. crit.*, 1974, p. 350.

[39] *A.P.*, Cases Nos. 1 and 2 under section 106 of the Works Constitution Act (BVG).

[40] R. Birk: "Auslandsbeziehungen und Betriebsverfassungsgesetz", in *Festschrift für Ludwig Schnorr von Carolsfeld* (Cologne, 1972); Walz, op. cit. in note 10. For an examination of the manner in which the concept of the "undertaking" may be interpreted in France to embrace groups, see A. Lyon-Caen: "Droit du travail et entreprises multinationales", in B. Goldmann and P. Francescakis (eds.): *L'Entreprise multinationale face au droit* (Paris, 1977).

[41] Text submitted by the Commission to the Council in 1980, in *Official Journal of the European Communities*, C. 297/1980. Summaries of parliamentary proceedings in *The Economist* (London), 16 Oct. 1982.

[42] See for example R. Birk: "Mitbestimmung und Kollisionsrecht", in *R.I.W./A.W.D.*, 1975, pp. 589 ff.

[43] *Neth. Yearb. Int. Law*, 1981, pp. 357-358; *Social and Labour Bul.*, 3/1981 and 2/1982. See also No. 1/1982 for a summary of a decision of the Labour Court of Amsterdam preventing the closing of a textile factory by a subsidiary of a group based in the Netherlands.

[44] See for example H. Bernstein and H. Koch: "Internationaler Konzern und deutsche Mitbestimmung", in *Z. ges. Handelsrecht*, 1979, pp. 522 ff.; C. Bellstedt: "Das territoriale Geltungsbereich des Mitbestimmungsgesetzes", in *Betr. Berat.*, 1977, pp. 1326-1329.

[45] For instance, a Spanish law of 1962, now repealed by the Workers' Charter of 1980, had a supplementary provision to the effect that it did not apply to undertakings whose principal place of business was abroad. In the Netherlands the legislation preserves the freedom of international companies to appoint and dismiss directors (See J. Maeijer: "Restructuration des entreprises commerciales dans la société industrielle commerciale", in *Rev. trim. droit commercial*, 1971, pp. 231 ff.). Norwegian legislation more generally makes possible exceptions if a company is associated with others in such a way as to make the system instituted by it inappropriate.

[46] As regards the Netherlands see Maeijer, op. cit.; as regards Spain under the former legislation, R. Birk: "Auf dem Weg zu einem einheitlichen europäischen Arbeitskollisionsrecht", in *N.J.W.*, 1978, pp. 1828 ff.

[47] See Bernstein and Koch, op. cit. in note 44.

[48] *A.P.*, Case No. 17 under "IPR Arbeitsrecht". At the same time the study cited in note 24 refers to cases in which detached workers are given the protection of the intervention of the works council by contract in circumstances in which the authority of the council might not extend to them by law.

[49] *IPRspr.*, 1979, No. 35.

[50] *Der Betrieb*, 1980, pp. 1030-1031.

[51] *A.P.*, Case No. 16 under "IPR Arbeitsrecht".

[52] *IPRspr.*, 1974, No. 43.

[53] See Birk, op. cit. in note 2.

[54] *IPRspr.*, 1979, No. 6.

[55] Some authors disagree, by reference to the purpose of such thresholds. However, the rule was upheld in the case cited in note 54.

[56] For a review of legislation up to 1970, see ILO: *Protection and facilities afforded to workers' representatives in the undertaking*, Report VIII (1), International Labour Conference, 54th Session, Geneva, 1970.

[57] However, disputes so settled may relate to matters abroad. This is expressly provided, in Great Britain, in section 126 A of the Employment Protection Act, 1975, as amended by the Employment Act, 1982.

[58] See for example F. Gamillscheg: *Internationales Arbeitsrecht* (Tübingen, 1959), at p. 366; A. Lyon-Caen: "La grève en droit international privé", in *Rev. crit.*, 1977, pp. 271 ff. One possible exception which has been cited is that of a self-contained group of workers of one nationality on a foreign worksite: see W. Gitter: "Probleme des Arbeitskampfs in supranationaler und internationalprivatrechtlicher Sicht", in *Z. f. Arbeitsrecht*, 1971, pp. 127 ff.

[59] *Rev. crit.*, 1970, pp. 684 ff.

[60] *Riv. dir. int. priv. proc.*, 1975, p. 131.

[61] See for example Gamillscheg, loc. cit. in note 58; C. Reithmann: *Internationales Vertragsrecht* (Cologne, 3rd ed., 1980); and Birk, op. cit. in note 46.

[62] See for example Lyon-Caen, op. cit. in note 58.

[63] 353 U.S. 138, *Int. Law Rep.*, Vol. 24, p. 167.

[64] 415 U.S. 104. The case is discussed by Maier: "Extraterritorial jurisdiction at a crossroads", in *Amer. J. Int. Law*, 1982, p. 280.

[65] *N.W.L. Ltd.* v. *Woods*, [1979] 3 All-E.R. 614.

[66] *The Camilla M*, [1979] 1 Lloyd's Rep. 26.

[67] *Arbeit u. Recht*, 1974, pp. 316 ff.

[68] ibid., 1977, pp. 254 ff.

[69] See A. Pankert: "Some legal problems of workers' international solidarity", in *Int. Labour Rev.*, July-Aug. 1977, pp. 67-74.

[70] ibid., at p. 72.

[71] *A.P.*, Case No. 20 under article 9 of the country's "basic law" (GG).

[72] In favour of the law where the primary action takes place, see for example Reithmann, op. cit. in note 61; in favour of that where the sympathy action is taken, see for example Pankert, op. cit. in note 69.

[73] R. Birk: "Grenzüberschreitende Streikabwehr", in *In memoriam Sir Otto Kahn-Freund* (Munich, 1980).

CONCLUSION

A comparative examination of existing material on the law applicable to employment relations with a foreign element leaves two quite distinct impressions.

The first impression is that under the rules of private international law there are two legal systems which have an important role to play in the labour field. One is that of the place of work: it is widely, though by no means universally, applied to the "typical" individual employment relation; its applicability is reinforced by the fact that much of it is mandatory; and without a doubt it is of prime importance in collective relations. The second of these legal systems is that of a home "base", often (though not necessarily) of both employer and employee: that system is applied not only to travelling personnel such as transport workers and to certain categories of mobile managerial staff but also to a considerable number of workers sent abroad for specific projects or assignments; certain connecting factors used to determine the law applicable to the "typical" employment relation (such as the common nationality or domicil of the parties, the place of business of the employer and even the place of conclusion of the contract) may lead to the adoption of that system; within limits, it can apply to collective as well as individual labour relations. Many of the conflicts and uncertainties inherent in the subject would seem to be due to the difficulty of establishing a clear dividing line between the legitimate scope of the law of the place of work and that of the home base (a difficulty compounded by such problems as that of identifying the true employer). The controverted issue of the choice of law by the parties may well be largely a reaction to that difficulty. Since there are already conflicts and uncertainty where these two basic systems confront each other, it is not surprising that the problems should be multiplied in cases in which a larger number of legal systems are involved, usually because there is no clear home base.

The second impression derived from a study of the subject is that in practice ways are being found of foreseeing and meeting at least some of the problems, although the relevant material has so far been little organised or examined. One solution may lie in agreements between a limited number of States on particular areas of collaboration, such as various co-operation agreements between socialist countries of Eastern Europe. Such international agreements may either lay down rules of private international law or specify substantive requirements which make choice of law superfluous: for instance, reference was made in Chapter II to bilateral agreements concerning construction works across frontiers; two of these laid down only rules of private international law; another (that governing work at Itaipú on the frontier between Brazil and Paraguay) mainly laid down rules of substantive law. Ways of avoiding, at least to some extent, conflicts of laws and uncertainty have no doubt been found also in some collective agreements for particular industries or particular undertakings, and in certain individual contracts of employment; a study published in the Federal Republic of Germany to which reference has been made in this survey in several contexts is a small beginning in the analysis of such material. Again, collective agreements or individual contracts can deal with the matter either through a choice of law or through the use of substantive provisions. In either case the agreement or contract needs to be based on a knowledge of the specific requirements, in private international law and in labour law, of the legal systems with a possible claim to applicability. Indeed, one characteristic of the various agreements and contracts mentioned in this paragraph may be, and may have to be, their specificity.

It has occasionally been suggested that in a field in which the problems are by definition international, a body such as the International Labour Organisation is particularly well placed to look into possible solutions. But what direction might such action take?

Another international organisation, the Hague Conference on Private International Law, is just beginning to consider the feasibility of a convention on the law applicable to the contract of employment. As indicated previously in several contexts, the European Communities have for some time had under consideration a draft regulation on an analogous subject. While the membership of the ILO is more extensive than that of either of those organisations, and standard-setting by them would not necessarily preclude the adoption of a further instrument by the ILO, it would seem to be preferable at this stage not to duplicate the preliminary consideration of the shape that might be given to such texts. A further point to be borne in mind is that a multilateral convention deriving its binding force from ratifications by individual States would require a long time at best to achieve the support necessary to affect a substantial number of employment relations and to generate faith in its practicability.

Moreover, while the unification or harmonisation of particular areas of labour law by means of international conventions may serve to avoid conflicts in those areas, it must be recalled that international labour standards have never been directed at such unification or harmonisation, but at setting minimum requirements.

A more promising aim may be to seek to further co-operation agreements among States, as well as collective agreements and individual contracts which avoid difficulties while protecting the parties, through the preparation of checklists of subjects to be covered, model clauses to deal with them and analogous guidance. It may moreover be desirable, given the differences in needs of different types of employment with foreign elements, that this should be done through the ILO's industrial activities in, for example, the building and civil engineering sector with regard to the detachment and hiring of workers for foreign construction sites, and the petroleum sector with regard to the legal provisions to be applied to offshore workers. As suggested above, effective progress may be directly related to the specificity of the means.

For this purpose a great deal more detailed information would need to be assembled. For instance, what are the dimensions of particular streams of what has been called "double migration", i.e. activities of an undertaking based in one country and operating in another, with labour conceivably hired in yet a third one? To what extent are the various matters which have been touched on in this survey dealt with in the contracts of the workers concerned? Are they covered by collective agreements, and if so which and how? Research on these subjects would require the co-operation of government departments, and above all of national and sectoral employers' and workers' organisations.

What may, then, be a prerequisite to progress is a wider awareness of the issues and the possibilities. Hitherto, because it is complex, private international law has largely been the preserve of a specialised group of lawyers. However, as suggested at the outset of this survey, it impinges on the work of persons concerned with the everyday administration and application of labour law. Some of the thought which the specialists have given to problems of conflicts of laws in labour matters needs to be translated into action at the practical level, and to receive the support or refutation that will stem from the resulting experience. In the absence of a sufficient body of clear rules, more bridges are needed between the lawyers who create conceptual models and the people confronted with the problems for which the models are intended to provide a solution. The present comparative survey is an attempt to contribute to this process of bridge-building.

SELECT BIBLIOGRAPHY

Battifol, H. "Projet de convention CEE sur la loi applicable aux obligations contractuelles." *Rev. trim. droit eur.*, 1975, pp. 181 ff.

Beitzke, G. "EWG-Kollisionsnormen zum Arbeitsverhältnis." In *Gedächtnisschrift für Rolf Dietz* (Munich, 1973).

– "Gerichtsstandsklauseln in auslandsbezogenen Dienst- und Arbeitsverträgen." *R.I.W./A.W.D.*, 1976, pp. 7 ff.

Bellstedt, C. "Das territoriale Geltungsbereich des Mitbestimmungsgesetzes." *Betr. Berat.*, 1977, pp. 1326-1329.

Bernstein, H., and Koch, H. "Internationaler Konzern und deutsche Mitbestimmung." *Z. f. ges. Handelsrecht*, 1979, pp. 522 ff.

Birk, R. "Auf dem Weg zu einem einheitlichen europäischen Arbeitskollisionsrecht." *N.J.W.*, 1978, pp. 1827 ff.

– "Auslandsbeziehungen und Betriebsverfassungsgesetz." In *Festschrift für Ludwig Schnorr von Carolsfeld* (Cologne, 1972).

– "Grenzüberschreitende Streikabwehr." In *In Memoriam Sir Otto Kahn-Freund* (Munich, 1980).

– "Internationales Tarifvertragsrecht." In *Festschrift für Günther Beitzke* (Berlin (West), 1978).

– "Mitbestimmung und Kollisionsrecht." *R.I.W./A.W.D.*, 1975, pp. 589 ff.

– "Multinational corporations and international labour law." In *International law problems of multinational corporations* (Heidelberg, 1978).

Blom, J. "Choice of law methods in the private international law of contract." *Can. Yearb. Int. Law*, 1978, pp. 230-275; 1979, pp. 206-246; 1980, pp. 161-200.

Bogouslavski, M. M. "Doctrine et pratique soviétique en droit international privé." *Cours Acad. droit int.*, 1981, I, pp. 335-431.

Buure-Hägglund, K. "Codification of private international law rules on employment contracts." *Scand. Studies in Law*, 1980.

Calleri, P. "Sulle norme de applicazione necessaria in materia di lavoro." *Riv. dir. int.*, 1970, pp. 551 ff.

Collins, L. "Contractual obligations: The EEC preliminary draft convention on private international law." *Int. Compar. Law Q.*, 1976, pp. 35 ff.

– "Exemption clauses, employment contracts and the conflict of laws." *Int. Compar. Law Q.*, 1972, pp. 320 ff.

Córdova, E. "Labour law aspects of frontier works: The Itaipú Dam case." *Int. Labour Rev.*, May-June 1976, pp. 303 ff.

Curti Gialdino, A. "La volonté des parties en droit international privé." *Cours Acad. droit int.*, 1972, III, pp. 751-921.

Däubler, W. "Grundprobleme des internationalen Arbeitsrechts." *A.W.D.*, 1972, pp. 8 ff.

– "Mitbestimmung und Betriebsverfassung im internationalen Privatrecht." *RabelsZ.*, 1975, pp. 444 ff.

– "Multinationale Konzerne und kollektives Arbeitsrecht." In Däubler-Wohlmuth: *Transnationale Konzerne und Weltwirtschaftsordnung* (Baden-Baden, 1978).

Deveali, M. L. "La relación de trabajo en el derecho internacional privado." *D° del trabajo*, 1952, p. 65.

Esko, T. *The law applicable to international labour relations*, Finnish national report to the 11th Congress of the International Academy of Comparative Law, Caracas, 1982.

Fenge, H. "Die betriebliche Altersversorgung im internationalen Privatrecht." *Der Betrieb*, 1976, pp. 51 ff.

Fermé, E. L. "Derecho internacional privado del trabajo." In A. Vasquez Vialard (ed.): *Tratado de derecho del trabajo*, Vol. II (Buenos Aires, 1982).

Fikentscher, W. "Arbeitsstatut, Prorogation und die zugehörigen Grenzen der Parteiautonomie." *Recht der Arbeit* (Munich), 1969, pp. 204-208.

Forde, M. "Transnational employment and employment protection." *Industr. Law J.*, 1978, pp. 228-238.

Foyer, J. "L'avant-projet de convention CEE sur la loi applicable aux obligations contractuelles et non contractuelles." *Clunet*, 1976, pp. 553 ff.

Francescakis, P. "Lois d'application immédiate et droit du travail." *Rev. crit.*, 1974, pp. 273-296.

Friedrich, K. "Probleme der Tarifverträge mit Auslandsberührungen." *Recht der Arbeit* (Munich), 1980, pp. 109 ff.

Gamillscheg, F. "Intereuropäisches Arbeitsrecht." *RabelsZ.*, 1973, pp. 284-316.

– *Internationales Arbeitsrecht* (Tübingen, 1959).

– "Neue Entwicklungen im englischen und europäischen internationalen Arbeitsrecht." *R.I.W./A.W.D.*, 1979, pp. 225 ff.

Garofalo, L. "Disciplina internazional-privatistica e prassi contratuale dei rapporti di lavoro in stato di *insulation*." *Riv. dir. int. priv. proc.*, 1976, pp. 756-781.

Gaudemet-Tallon, H. "Le nouveau droit international privé des contrats." *Rev. trim. droit eur.*, 1981, pp. 215-285.

Geefken, R. "Internationales Recht im Seeleutestreik." *N.J.W.*, 1979, pp. 1739 ff.

Geppert, W. "Arbeitsverhältnis und arbeitsbezogene Vorschriften im internationalen Privatrecht." *Das Recht der Arbeit* (Vienna), 1970, pp. 124-143, 259-274.

Gitter, W. "Probleme des Arbeitskampfs in supranationaler und international-privatrechtlicher Sicht." *Z. f. Arbeitsrecht*, 1971, pp. 127 ff.

Giuliano, M., and Lagarde, P. "Report on the Convention on the Law Applicable to Contractual Obligations." *Official Journal of the European Communities*, C. 282/1980.

Goldschmidt, W. "Derecho internacional privado del trabajo." In M. Deveali (ed.): *Tratado de derecho del trabajo*, Vol. IV (Buenos Aires, 1966), Book X.

Guzman, R. A., and Iturraspe, F. J. Paper in *El derecho venezolano en 1982* (national report to the 11th Congress of the International Academy of Comparative Law, Caracas, 1982).

Hepple, B. A. "Conflicts of laws in employment relationships within the EEC." In K. Lipstein (ed.): *Harmonisation of private international law by the EEC* (London, 1978).

von Hoffmann, B. "Über den Schutz des Schwächeren bei internationalen Schuldverträgen." *RabelsZ.*, 1974, pp. 396 ff.

Isele, H. G. "Auslandsmontage im Arbeitsrecht." In *Festschrift für H. G. Ficker* (Frankfurt am Main, 1967).

Kahn-Freund, O. "Delictual liability and the conflict of laws." *Cours Acad. droit int.*, 1968, II, pp. 1 ff.

– "General problems of private international law." ibid., 1974, III.

Kitchen, J. *Labour law and offshore oil* (London, 1977).

Kopelmanas, L. "L'application du droit national aux sociétés multinationales." *Cours Acad. droit int.*, 1976, II.

Knapp, B. "La protection des travailleurs des sociétés membres du groupe." In *Colloque international sur le droit international privé des groupes de sociétés* (Geneva, 1973).

Kronke, H. *Rechtstatsachen, kollisionsrechtliche Methodenentfaltung und Arbeitnehmerschutz im internationalen Arbeitsrecht* (Tübingen, 1980).

– "Europäische Vereinheitlichung des Arbeitskollisionsrechts als Wirtschafts- und Sozialpolitik." *RabelsZ.*, 1981, pp. 301-319.

Kropholler, J. "Das kollisionsrechtliche System des Schutzes der schwächeren Vertragspartei." *RabelsZ.*, 1978, pp. 634-661.

Lagarde, P. "'Dépeçage' dans le droit international privé des contrats." *Riv. dir. int. priv. proc.*, 1975, pp. 649 ff.

Lalive, P. Reports on the application of foreign public law (in French), in *Ann. Inst. droit int.*, 1975.

Lando, O. "Les obligations contractuelles." In *European private international law of obligations* (Tübingen, 1975).

Leffler, F. "Das Recht der Flagge im internationalen Seearbeitsrecht." *Recht der Arbeit* (Munich), 1978, pp. 97-101.

Lipstein, K. "Inherent limitations in statutes and the conflict of laws." *Int. Compar. Law Q.*, 1977, pp. 884 ff.

Loussouarn, Y. "La convention de La Haye sur la loi applicable en matière d'accidents de la circulation routière." *Clunet*, 1969, pp. 5-21.

– "La convention de La Haye sur la loi applicable à la responsabilité du fait des produits." *Clunet*, 1974, pp. 32 ff.

Lyon-Caen, A. "Droit du travail et entreprises multinationales." In B. Goldman and P. Francescakis (eds.): *L'entreprise multinationale face au droit* (Paris, 1977).

– "La grève en droit international privé." *Rev. crit.*, 1977, pp. 271 ff.

– "La mise à disposition internationale de salariés." *Droit social*, 1981, pp. 747 ff.

– "Rapports internationaux de travail." ibid., 1978, pp. 197-203.

Lyon-Caen, G. "La convention collective de travail en droit international privé." *Clunet*, 1964, pp. 247 ff.

– "Négociation et convention collective au niveau européen." *Rev. trim. droit eur.*, 1973, pp. 583 ff. and 1974, pp. 1 ff.

– "Observations sur le licenciement dans les groupes internationaux de sociétés." *Rev. crit.*, 1974, pp. 439 ff.

Lyon-Caen, G. and A. *Droit social international et européen* (Paris, 5th ed., 1980).

Maeijer, J. "Restructuration des entreprises commerciales dans la société industrielle commerciale." *Rev. trim. droit commercial*, pp. 231 ff.

Makarov, A. N. *Quellen des internationalen Privatrechts*, Vol. I (Tübingen, 3rd ed., 1978).

Malintoppi, A. "Norme di applicazione necessaria e norme di diritto internazionale privato in materia di lavoro." *Riv. dir. int.*, 1962, pp. 278 ff.

Mann, F. A. "Statutes and the conflict of laws." *Brit. Yearb. Int. Law.* 1972-73, pp. 117 ff.

Mari, L. "Rapporti di lavoro, principi constituzionali e deroga alle giurisdizioni secondo la Convenzione di Bruxelles del 1968." *Riv. dir. int. priv. proc.*, 1981, pp. 51-84.

Mayer, P. "Les lois de police étrangères." *Clunet*, 1981, pp. 277 ff.

Morgenstern, F., and Knapp, B. "Multinational enterprises and the extraterritorial application of labour law." *Int. Compar. Law Q.*, 1978, pp. 769-793.

Müller, G. "Die rechtliche Behandlung abhängiger fremdbestimmter Arbeit bei Berührung mit Deutschland und Italien." *Recht der Arbeit* (Munich), May-June 1973.

Northstein, G. Z., and Ayres, J. P. "The multinational corporation and the extraterritorial application of the Labor-Management Relations Act." *Cornell Int. Law J.*, Vol. 10, pp. 1-58.

Oppetit, B. "Groupes de sociétés et droit du travail." *Rev. des sociétés*, 1973, pp. 69 ff.

Panebianco, M. *Lo statuto dei lavoratori italiani all'estero* (Naples, 1974).

Pankert, A. "Some legal problems of workers' international solidarity." *Int. Labour Rev.*, July-Aug. 1977, pp. 67-74.

Piron, J. "Eléments de réflexion pour la solution des conflits de lois en matière de droit du travail." *Droit social*, 1966, pp. 212 ff.

Philip, A. "Contracts of employment in the law of conflict of laws of the EEC." In *International law and economic order* (Munich, 1977).

Pocar, F. "Jurisdiction and the enforcement of judgements under the EEC Convention of 1968." *RabelsZ.*, 1978, pp. 405 ff.

– "La legge applicabile ai rapporti di lavoro secondo il diritto italiano." *Riv. dir. int. priv. proc.*, 1972, pp. 726-754.

– "Norme di applicazione necessaria e conflitti di leggi in tema di rapporti di lavoro." ibid., 1967, pp. 734-744.

Reithmann, C. *Internationales Vertragsrecht* (Cologne, 3rd ed., 1980).

Rodière, P. *La convention collective de travail et le droit international* (thesis, University of Paris I, 1977).

– "Le projet européen de règlement uniforme des conflits de lois en matière de relations de travail." *Rev. trim. droit eur.*, 1973, pp. 1-28.

Rojot, J. *International collective bargaining* (Deventer, 1978).

Russomano, G. M. C. *Direito internacional privado do trabalho* (Rio de Janeiro, 2nd ed., 1979).

Savatier, J. "Les groupes de sociétés et la notion d'entreprise en droit du travail." In *Etudes de droit du travail offertes à André Brun* (Paris, 1974).

Schnorr, G. *Arbeits- und sozialrechtliche Fragen der europäischen Integration* (Berlin (West), 1974).

– "Aspekte des internationalen Privatrechts der gewerbsmässigen Arbeitnehmerüberlassung." *Z. f. Arbeitsrecht*, 1975, pp. 143 ff.

Schwarz, H. "Problematik internationaler Arbeitsverträge für deutsche Arbeitnehmer in Brasilien." *R.I.W./A.W.D.*, 1976, pp. 50 ff.

Simitis, S. "Internationales Arbeitsrecht – Standort und Perspektiven." In *Festschrift für Gerhard Kegel* (Frankfurt am Main, 1977).

Simon-Depitre, M. "Droit du travail et conflits de lois." *Rev. crit.*. 1958, pp. 285 ff.

– "La loi du 3 janvier 1972 sur le travail temporaire et le droit international privé." ibid., 1973, pp. 277 ff.

Smith, R. "International employment contracts: Contracting out." *Int. Compar. Law Q.*, 1972, pp. 164 ff.

Szaszy, I. *Conflict of laws in the Western, socialist and developing countries* (Leyden, 1974).

– "Conflicts between labour statutes of a public law character." In *Scritti in onore di Gaspare Ambrosini* (Milan, 1970).

– *International labour law* (Leyden, 1968).

– Reports on conflicts of laws in labour matters (in French). *Ann. Inst. droit int.*, 1971.

Thomson, J. M. "International employment contracts: The Scottish approach." *Int. Compar. Law Q.*, 1974, p. 458.

Vacarie, I. *L'employeur* (Paris, 1979).

Valladão, H. *Direito internacional privado*, Vol. III (Rio de Janeiro, 1978), Ch. LXVI.

Vannes, V. "Droit applicable au contrat de travail en présence d'éléments d'extranéité." *J. Trib. Travail*, 1981, pp. 237-240.

Vincent, J. "Quelques observations sur les conflits de juridictions en matière de contrat de travail." In *Etudes de droit du travail offertes à André Brun* (Paris, 1974), pp. 603-617.

Vischer, F. "The antagonism between legal security and the search for justice." *Cours Acad. droit int.*, 1974, II, pp. 1-65.

Walz, S. *Multinationale Unternehmen und internationaler Tarifvertrag* (Baden-Baden, 1981).